Heart, Laughter, and Sentiment

Heart, Laughter, and Sentiment

Poems and Short Stories for Your Every Day

Eugene Pacetti and
Jessica Robin Cooper

iUniverse, Inc.
New York   Bloomington

iUniverse books may be ordered through booksellers or by contacting:

iUniverse
1663 Liberty Drive
Bloomington, IN 47403
www.iuniverse.com
1-800-Authors (1-800-288-4677)

Because of the dynamic nature of the Internet, any Web addresses or links contained in this book may have changed since publication and may no longer be valid. The views expressed in this work are solely those of the author and do not necessarily reflect the views of the publisher, and the publisher hereby disclaims any responsibility for them.

ISBN: 978-1-4401-3807-2 (sc)
ISBN: 978-1-4401-3808-9 (ebook)

Printed in the United States of America

iUniverse rev. date: 10/22/2009

Preface

Over the years I have written poems and short stories about events that have happened in my life. I would then tuck them away and forget about them. When I was a para professional at school, I would write poems and stories and read them to the students. Some poems would be about the teachers or students themselves.

People would ask me for a copy of the poem I wrote and suggested I publish a book. I finally took their advice and compiled some short stories and poems my granddaughter and I wrote and put them together in a book.

I hope these short stories and poems put a little enjoyment in your life.

Section One:

Short Stories

SPRING SYMPHONY

By Jessica Robin Cooper

When I was a little girl we lived in the country, on a hill. In today's hustle and bustle world, at times, when I'm at home, I sit back close my eyes and think of the wonderful days when I was a kid.

I know that spring is here when I relax peacefully in the chaos of my yard with the hot sunshine beating on my face. As I lie there staring at the puffy white clouds in the sky, I always try to figure out what shapes they are making. As a cloud floats by, it slowly separates into a hundred pieces, giving the appearance of little frogs that are hopping in our newly dug pond. Then, all they do is sit and croak all night, usually keeping me up.

As I close my eyes I hear the beautiful song of a bird. His music is much more beautiful than that of the frogs. When I open my eyes I notice him. The chickadee, no bigger than my hand, black with a yellow belly and white between his eyes, sits pecking at the black oil sunflower bell hanging from my mother's carefully constructed bird habitat in the back yard.

Just below him, a short distance from the feeder is a robin, rusty brown belly with a black back that shines blue in the sunlight, struggling and tugging on a worm that won't come out of its hole. She can't let go. She needs this worm to feed her babies, which are only a hop, skip and a short fly away. I'm thinking, I wish I could help her. Then she does it. Out pops the worm, and away the robin flies to her nest. As I watch her feed her newborn babies, I notice, out of the corner of my eye, a hummingbird, bright green with purples and blues like a peacock with it's tail open, sucking sweet nectar out of the red feeder my mom has hung by the bay window. I turn slowly, listening to the hum of his wings, not wanting to scare him; then in a flash he was gone.

As I sit up, a cool spring breeze catches the white fluffy dandelions and blows them across the yard as if it were snowing. Amidst all the dandelion snow, a red squirrel, with a big puffy tail, digs in the feeder, like a dog, trying to pick just the pieces of the food he wants, throwing the rest on the ground. Mom's going to be mad.

Meanwhile, another robin is busy collecting material for a nest she is building in my handmade birdhouse, which I put in a tree next to the pond. It's amazing. For weeks I have been watching her carry many different supplies to build her humble abode. String, hay, moss, and fresh cut grass are just a few of the pieces she is using.

These sights are just a few of the delightful momentary memories that I am able to enjoy in the comfort of my home. The smell of the fresh cut grass, the pesky squirrels, the birds hard at work, and the frogs hopping around the pond are just a few of the obvious signs that spring is in full swing.

Early in the evening, as I sit on our back deck, I watch the deer come out of the woods. There's a mother deer with her little fawn. Well that's another story.

SUMMER SENSATIONS

By Jessica Robin Cooper

The coming of summer brings the sensation that will tickle your taste buds, a deeper red than the ripest cherry. Fields are lined with the appearance of jewels from afar. As you gently lift a runner, the sweetest upended dewdrop dangles—a STRAWBERRY. Berry picking is an unforgettable summertime experience.

The art of strawberry picking has been passed from generation to generation in our family. This art starts by choosing the perfect day and time to embark on our journey. Either at dawn, as the sun begins to rise in the east and the morning dew begins to distill, or at dusk, when the orange semicircle peeks over the mountains to devote just enough light, is the best time to pick each and every red ripened strawberry.

The number one rule I was taught in picking berries is to periodically test the exquisite taste to determine if you are picking the crème of the crop. The proper way to fully taste the berry is to place the entire fruit into your mouth. Do not chew; instead squish it to the roof of your mouth, allowing the sweet nectar to saturate your taste buds. Then ask yourself, "Is this the taste I'm looking for?" If not, move to another area and run a taste test once again. Remember all of the strawberries you eat during the field test are free. So eat, eat, and eat while you can. When you have the perfect flavor then fill your container to the top. Your container should be a cardboard flat or a wooden basket to allow the maximum amount of air to reach your gems.

The more you pick the longer you will enjoy them. Also remember to carefully pluck these precious jewels from the runners and place them into your container, as not to damage the goods, or you might have to indulge on the spot. When your belly is full and the basket is overflowing, it's time to head for home.

During the ride home you imagine all of the delicious delights you will be enjoying from your berries. Some we will freeze for those cold winter months, others we will remember every morning as we spread them on our toast as jam. A bowl full should be placed in the refrigerator for snacks, while the rest will be tonight's desert—strawberry shortcake with a little ice cream. Before the summer is over we will enjoy another trip to the strawberry patch to fill our baskets and our bellies once again.

HOW POSSUM TROT GOT IT'S NAME

By Eugene Pacetti

Back in the 1800's my great granddaddy lived off Spring Hill Road, just outside of Lewisburg, TN, on one of the S curves that go up the mountain. Back then this area was called The Community. Now he and my great Uncle Buford had two big barns where they raised opossums. One barn was opossums for the dinner table and the other barn they raised opossums for racing.

On the first Saturday of each month The Community held their opossum races getting ready for the big event of the year, The Annual Possum Festival, held in September, which included the big opossum race to determine who would be the year's Possum King.

On one of the S turns was The Communities big general store and next to the store was The Community Pavilion. At the back of the pavilion was a big kitchen where all the opossum meat was prepared for market.

But in September everything focused on the Annual Possum Trot Fall Festival, and the kitchen was busy preparing opossum for the big possum feast and dance that would be held after the big possum race, and king possum would be crowned. If you travel up the mountain, as you go around the S curves, you can still see the two big barns where they raised opossums.

There's a new general store where the old store used to be, and as you go around one of those S curves you'll see a big sign on the side of the store that reads, POSSUM TROT GENERAL STORE.

Now the racetrack was on the other side of the road and set down in a holler. The bank around the racetrack provided excellent seating, and a good view for all to see the big race. The Possum Trot Fall Festival was the biggest event in Marshall County.

It drew people from miles around all hoping their possum would win the big race and they would be crowned King Possum.

The Festival started early in the morning with a possum sausage and pancake breakfast.

After breakfast the men would ready their possum for a day of racing. Each possum had its own little colored vest, with a white number on the back, representing the owner.

While the men were running their qualifying races, the women were in the big kitchen preparing the big possum feast to be held that evening. There would be a dance and King Possum would be crowned.

The big feast would include fried possum legs, deep fried livers and gizzards. There were possum breast strips rolled in corn meal and there were possum burgers for the kids. There was also possum pie and hot possum chili. Of course no meal would be complete with out mashed potatoes and hot possum gravy.

Preliminary races would go on all day. There were ten races with ten possums to a race. The ten winners would then race for the racing championship and the owner would be crowned King Possum. A trophy was awarded to the winner and King Possum would receive $100.00 in cash. This was a large amount of money back in the 1800's.

Each year the Festival got bigger and bigger and drew people, not only from Marshall County, but from all over Tennessee. People coming in to Lewisburg would ask how to get to the races and where was the possum trot festival?

Well a sign was put up on the corner of Springplace Road and the main road, which is now N. Ellington Pike, which read THIS WAY TO POSSUM TROT. The name stuck and that's how this little community got its name.

Well, it was the fall of 1883 that will live in infamy. The Festival was in full swing on this September morning. People had set up booths to sell their homemade goodies, like jams, pickles, pies and cakes. The qualifying races had started and everyone looked forward to the banquet and dance that evening.

This year there were 100 possums entered, the most ever. There would be 10 possums to a race and there would be 10 races. The ten winners would then race for the championship to see who would be crowned King Possum. The winner would receive a big trophy and $500.00 cash, which was a lot of money in those days.

After the races everyone would gather at the big pavilion for the annual possum banquet and the awarding of prizes and to crown King Possum. After the banquet they would dance the night away, and the most popular song was called Possum Trot. Today the words are different but the tune is the same,

(sing to the tune of Rocky Top).
Wish I was back in Possum Trot,
Down in the Tennessee hills.
Ain't no smog around ole Possum Trot,
Don't have a telephone bill.
Once I had a girl in Possum Trot,
Courted her in the dark.
Big as a buck but sweet as a still.
I always dream about her,
Possum Trot you'll always be,
Home sweet home to me.
Good ole Possum Trot.
Possum Trot Tennessee,
Possum Trot Tennessee.

The daily races had concluded and my great granddaddy and my Uncle Buford both had a possum in the final race of the day. Naturally they both thought they had a good chance to be crowned King Possum. Not only was the title at stake but the winner could get either stud fees or big money for the baby possums of the winner.

The big bell on top of the pavilion rang; it was time for the big race of the day.

The final ten possums were getting ready. All had their vest on, with the white number on top. There would be no doubt which possum crossed the finish line first. The bank around the oval race track was crowed with spectators, yelling for their favorite possum.

Great granddaddy was getting nervous; this was the first year his possum was in the final race. He slipped out his little jug of Tennessee white lightning and took a sip to settle his nerves. Then he got a brilliant idea; he gave his little possum a sip, just to loosen him up. My great Uncle Buford just happen to be in the stalls and saw what was going on. He figured two could play this game, and he gave his possum a sip of good ole Tennessee mountain dew.

Some how, maybe it was the smell of the home brew, the other eight racers figured out what was going on. And wouldn't you know it, they all soused up their possums.

Just then the starter called out, "Everyone ready their possum for the race, get 'em to the starting line."

The possums were placed in their starting stalls, all was ready. The starter raised his pistol and BANG the race was on. The final race would be two laps around the oval. The possums took off like a streak and they were all bunched up as they rounded the first turn. Coming down the back stretch they started to spread out, and as they completed the first lap four possums were running side by side. Then great granddaddy and Uncle Buford's possums started to move ahead. All of a sudden they started to weave and wander back and forth across the track. As they came to the turn they hit the fence and broke it down. Out through the field they ran as the other possums followed weaving and tumbling as they went.

(sing to the tune of Battle of New Orleans)
They ran through the bushes,
And they ran through the woods.
Ran through the briars,
Where the men couldn't go.
They ran so fast,
The hounds couldn't catch 'em.
Down Snake Creek,
All the way to Lewisburg.

My great Uncle Buford was fuming, he just knew he would be this year's King Possum. He went up to great granddaddy's barn and turned all his possums loose. Well, great granddaddy was doing the same thing to great Uncle Buford. With all the excitement, no one was watching the kitchen, then some one yelled, "The kitchen's on fire." With all the grease in the kitchen, the building burned hot and fast. It quickly spread to the pavilion and before long all was lost.

This was the last of the big possum races and there would be no more Possum Festivals. The song, the dance, and the Possum Trot was lost forever. But when you go to a dance and someone does the buck dance or a group begins to clog, and the tune is Rocky Top. Sure sounds like Possum Trot to me. When you're out driving at night, every once in a while, all over Tennessee, you might see a possum racing across the highway. Could they be descendants of the famous racing possums of POSSUM TROT??

THE TRIANGLE

By Jessica Robin Cooper

The truth was finally expressed on one beautiful summer Sunday afternoon as the trail abruptly came to an end. Matthew and Dawn found themselves staring at a sparkling brook. Rolling over the stones, the brook was perfectly accented by the glaring high noon sun. They packed a picnic lunch to enjoy the great outdoors and the perfect weather. They spread their blanket and brought out their lunch. Matthew noticed an eagle high above. The eagle flew down and landed on a broken tree branch sticking out of the brook. Matthew didn't seem concerned with the eagle. Dawn noticed a small triangular patch of brown on the eagle's forehead.

"Matthew, look at the mark on the eagle's head."

"I've seen that same eagle before!" Matthew exclaimed enthusiastically.

"When did you see it before?"

Matthew began to tell of the last encounter with the same eagle. "Well ever since I was about ten and a half, my father and I would go on Sunday afternoon walks in the …"

"In these same woods, right? Did you pack a picnic like this too?" Dawn rudely interjected.

"Yes, it was in these same woods. No, we never packed a picnic lunch. Now will you let me finish what I was saying?"

"Yeah, yeah, go on."

"Thank you. As I was saying, we would go on walks in these woods. The funny thing was we never found this brook until I was about twelve."

As he continued to tell his story the eagle flew over and landed unsurprising on a rock next to Matthew.

"Not only did I discover the brook but lying next to it was an eagle…"Matthew stated excitedly. I turned to my father and said, "He looks hurt. Is there anything we can do to help him?" My dad told me that we could bring him back to the house.

"The other animals in the pasture were getting jealous because I was spending so much time in the loft helping the eagle mend his wing. We kept him in the barn for a little over a month. Then one day we released him from the loft. He soared off into the blue. I didn't think he would ever come back," Matthew stopped with a tear in his eye.

"That's very touching and I'm glad you had a chance to share it with me. I have just one question."

"Go ahead, Dawn, what is it?"

"Does he stay hear year round or does he migrate in the winter?"

"Dream, which is the name I've given him, stays in the loft during the winter or he nestles with any of the half dozen cattle or even one of the two horses."

Now, even three years after the accident, Matthew and Dream come down to the brook side to comfort each other as well as to talk. Sometimes Matthew has a hard time talking to a friend or parent so he confides in Dream. Matthew knows that Dream can't talk back to him but he listens attentively as if there were no distractions. Dream is like the best friend everyone wishes for. He never disagrees.

"Well it's getting late. Do you think we should pick up and head for home?" asked Matthew.

"Yeah, let's get going. I think tomorrow is a big day. Do you think so?"

"Yes, the first day of high school will be a challenge."

They began their walk back and Dream followed them all the way. When they reached the barn, the eagle flew into the loft to call it a night. Matthew and Dawn went into the house and Dawn called her mom to come pick her up. Matthew's mom noticed tears in their eyes. She bluntly said, "It was the story of Dream, now wasn't it?"

"Yes it was very touching, Matthew; my mom will be here in twenty minutes. Was that all to the story?" she asked.

"Matthew, did you tell Dawn the Indian legend behind the story?" his mom asked curiously.

"No."

"Tell me, I want to know."

Matthew and Dawn went upstairs to his room so he could show her the pictures that went with this legend. Just as they began to talk about it Dawn's mother was there to take her home.

"We'll have to talk about this again soon," stated Dawn as she hurried down the stairs.

"Okay, see you tomorrow."

MATTHEW'S LEGEND

The eagle is the symbol of pride. Having pride does not mean to be stubborn. Throughout this experience Matthew noticed that the eagle, Dream, was proud that someone was there to help him. Dream wasn't stubborn. He let Matthew and his father help to mend his wing. Dream was able to accept the fact that without the help of Matthew he probably would not be flying today. Matthew also noticed that Dream showed his appreciation by staying close to his house and to him.

Matthew gave him the name Dream from his experience as a young child. When he was younger he always dreamed of helping an animal that was hurt. Since his dream had come true he felt that was the name that fit perfectly. His dream had become a reality.

LIFE AMONG THE TREES

By Jessica Robin Cooper

"Good morning Majestico. My, you must have grown three feet this summer."

"Why thank you sweet thing. You aren't looking bad yourself. Your leaves are turning rich shades of red and yellow."

The majestic spruce stood tall as he fluffed his brows. He always referred to Mapleene as sweet thing because every spring as the farmer tapped her bark to start the sweet sap running he would say, "This maple tree gives the sweetest syrup of all in the mountains."

"Mapleene, I think this is the year."

"Year for what?" she asked.

"This is the year I could stand tall in Boston; maybe even around the rink at Rockefeller Plaza or, best of all, atop the hill in front of the White House, for the president."

"Wow!" exclaimed Mapleene, "Where would you like to go the most?"

"Well…" he pauses for a moment.

"Come on," she said, "I really want to know."

"It would be an honor to serve the president at the White House or over look the ocean from the Boston Common, but the best place of all would be Rockefeller Center."

"Why?"

"Capturing the priceless memories of couples walking by hand in hand without a care in the world, or watching children on the ice tumbling and laughing as they take a few spills learning how to skate—that is how I would love to spend Christmas. Can you imagine the thousands of lights reflecting from the icicles that would form on my branches, and the many feet of garland encircling my body and the countless ornaments carefully placed upon my branches depicting the joyous season."

"That sounds wonderful," sighed Mapleene.

"I have had this dream since I was a tiny fir."

Mapleene was excited as she exclaimed, "Since I was a sapling I have dreamed of becoming a beautifully carved bedroom set, or a handcrafted executive desk given as a gift on Christmas morning to the president of the United States. I can see it now, carefully hand carved maple leaves etched across the front. At the bottom of each corner a leaf touched in red and gold, symbolizing my bold fall colors. The drawer pulls would be antique brass leaves and across the long middle drawer, an articulate string of tiny maple trees. Finally, as you slide open the drawer, carefully inscribed in the front right corner reads, 'This Maple Tree Grew in Vermont'."

"Great," roars Majestico, and the star placed upon my top shall rise to the sky and shine brightly as it did when it lead the Wise men."

"Hush Majestico, listen. Someone is coming."

Unknown to the two beautiful species, a gorgeous maple hardwood and gigantic spruce softwood, the people who would make their dreams come true were near. Now, many years later, as Mapleleen sits as the desk under the hand of the president in the White House and Majestico watches from the edge of the ice in Rockefeller Center, what they left behind on the edge of a mountain hiking trail in Vermont has begun to grow into new dreams.

HOW DO YOU PUNISH AN ANGEL?

By Eugene Pacetti

This is for the grandparents who have had a grandchild visit for the weekend. God bless the little ones. They want to go to Grandma's because she makes good stuff to eat or they want to go to Papa's because he takes them to the store.

All week long my granddaughter, Jessica, (now Jessica Robin Cooper) who was 12 at the time, had planned on spending the weekend with my wife and I. Why was this weekend such a big deal? My wife was going to show her how to make cinnamon buns. Now, my wife's cinnamon buns were the talk of the town. They were big, fluffy light in texture, with a flavor out of this world. They were known all over as "Julia's Buns."

We picked Jessica up early Saturday morning and we were off to the grocery store where her grandmother would show her all the ingredients needed for making cinnamon buns. After grocery shopping we headed for the clothing store. Jessica got a pair of jeans and a shirt and she picked out some jeans and a shirt for her sister, who was at home. We made a habit never to buy for one and not the other.

We dropped gram off at home and Jessica and I headed for the hobby shop. She was going to build a miniature solar car and race it. This was a big school project which would turn out to be a state and a New England event. After a fast food lunch we headed home and to the basement and my workshop. (This is another story you can read)

After supper Jessica and her grandmother occupied the kitchen and turned out some of the best cinnamon buns you ever put in your mouth. The smell of those buns permeated the entire house. These were to be the highlight of Sunday brunch.

Sunday morning and we were off to church, but not before we sampled those cinnamon buns. After church it was my job to fix brunch, I would have eggs, bacon, sausage, home fries, toast, and hot coffee or hot cocoa.

While I was getting everything ready, Jessica went to the bathroom to put on her new clothes. She came into the kitchen and asked, "Papa can I help?" I said, "Sure you can, get the eggs and the butter out of the refrigerator. Then you can make the toast."

The bacon was sizzling in the pan, when I heard my wife holler from the bathroom, "Hon, the bathroom is flooding." I ran down the hall into the bathroom, slipped, fell on the floor and slid into the toilet. I shut the water off, then heard a scream from the kitchen, "Gram, the bacon's burning and its smoking." When my wife got to the smoked filled kitchen the bacon was burned to a crisp. She turned off the stove, opened the window, turned on the overhead fan.

Meanwhile back in the bathroom I was using the plunger to unplug the toilet with no luck. I then took a metal coat hanger, straightened it out, leaving the hook on the end. I proceeded to poke the coat hanger down the toilet and I was pulling out gobs of toilet paper that didn't dissolve. After I pulled out a big gob, I used the plunger and it all broke free and the toilet was now flushing again. I poured some drain opener down the toilet to dissolve any paper that might be stuck in the pipes. I took a quick shower, changed my clothes and headed to the kitchen to check out the smoke situation.

When I entered the kitchen I got the surprise of my life, Brunch was all cooked and Jessica said, "I helped cook Papa, and we did your eggs over easy, just like you like them." After a delicious brunch, which included a cinnamon bun, Jessica gave me a big hug and said, "I'm sorry Papa, I love you." HOW DO YOU PUNISH AN ANGEL?

GOOD DEEDS ARE ALWAYS REPAID

By Jessica Robin Cooper

It was just five days before Christmas when the snow began falling in the town of Sugarplum. On a vacant street through the center of town a ragged old man lay stranded alone. His life was rough without any money. The hunger was tearing at his insides. He got up from his bed of cardboard boxes and newspapers thinking of where his next meal would come from. Slowly he walked across the street to the diner. Soon many people would be coming to the diner for breakfast. Surely, he thought, someone would have a little Christmas spirit and perhaps provide him with a cup of coffee and a doughnut. As he sat to rest on the entrance steps of the diner, a young couple approached him.

"Are you all right sir?" asks the young man.

"Yes, thank you for asking," the older gentleman replied.

"Have you had any breakfast on this cold morning?" asked the young lady.

"No, I just crawled out of my box."

"My wife and I would love it if you would join us for breakfast."

"Thank you that would be wonderful."

As the three of them entered the diner, heads turned and all eyes were fixed on the old man. The waitress seated them at a booth near the window. The speedy service of the waitress allowed them to slowly enjoy their Christmas breakfast. After a delicious and filling meal the older gentleman retrieved a name card and pen from his pocket.

"I want to thank you for your generosity and kindness. Could I please have your name and address? One day I will repay you."

"Being the Christmas season we couldn't have anything better for a nicer person," said the young man, "It would be my pleasure to give it to you."

The old man departed and they each went their separate ways not knowing if their paths would ever cross again.

Five years have passed since that memorable breakfast on that December 20th day. For the past four years on this same day the young couple received a Christmas card with a certified check for one thousand dollars.

The mailman was arriving and the day is December 20th. The young couple anxiously awaited the mail. Would they receive the same unmarked Christmas card this year with another one thousand dollars? As they looked through the letters, there it was the same type Christmas card they had received for the past four years. As they opened the card there it was, a certified check for one thousand dollars.

Where did it come from? Who sent it? Could it be the old man they shared breakfast with five years ago? They probably will never know. There is an old proverb that states, "A good deed will be repaid a hundred fold."

A RACE TO REMEMBER

By: Jessica Robin Cooper

Image the exhilaration of winning a big race-not a road race, but a car race. Not a real car, but a model solar car you built yourself. While only in the seventh grade I had a chance to build a car that would run on solar energy. One day a man came to our school and introduced us to the Junior Solar Sprint program. We would be able to purchase a solar panel and a small motor. We then would design and build a solar car to race. There would be races in our area, then to state competition and on to the New England regional's. There I was with a solar panel to power my small motor and a wondering imagination of what my car would look like. I had two goals in mind, first was winning the races and the second was the design.

The first thing I had to do was draw a sketch of my car so it would meet the physical requirements. The specifications were strict, it could only be thirty centimeters long, it was not to exceed fifteen centimeters high, it had to be able to carry an empty soda can, and it had to have two eye hooks on the bottom, one centimeter from the ground to run on a guide wire. These requirements didn't seem hard to meet; the question I pondered in my mind was what material I would use to construct the body.

I needed a light weight but durable material; I decided to ask my grandfather, Papa, for advice. He took me to the local hobby shop where we found many different things to use. The store owner showed me one that most people use for model ships, planes and cars; balsa wood. It was light, flexible and durable, so I decided to use it. Now I had materials and a plan; it was time to implement them. I would choose the wheels after the body was built, everything had to be precise.

It was only three months until the local area competition and I spent all my spare time at Papa's house building the body that had to be streamlined with little wind resistance. This was a racer with style. I made the front panel tapered to a twenty-two degree angle, up to the fifteen centimeter height requirement. I cut a hole in the front panel and left the rear end open so the air would flow through freely. A little sanding in the front and rear and it was thirty centimeters long. This was it! It had the appearance of an Indy car. The solar panel would be fastened to the top and the drive wheels would be in the rear. My design was perfect. This was the car to win!

Papa and I went back to the hobby shop where we found the perfect set of wheels. I mounted the motor with a pulley on the shaft and aligned it with the pulley on the axle to the wheel. Everything looked good. We took my car to a factory parking lot and set up a guide wire. A piece of cardboard covered the solar panel to prevent the sun from running the motor. Hooked it to the guide wire, removed the cardboard and away she went. Wow, it ran perfect. We ran a few more test runs and thought we were ready for the local race.

Finally the day was here, and we got to miss classes to go to the race. It was a dark overcast day and I wasn't sure if we were going to race at all. I had worked so hard, I didn't want to go home. The races were to start at 9 a.m., but no such luck. It was 10:30 a.m. and the sun broke through the clouds. It was announced that the races would start at 11 a.m.

I did well for the first three rounds and I was in the semifinals. I waited for my heat and I was assigned to lane three. When the cars were called to the line I got butterflies in my stomach. I set my car on the guide wire and waited for the popgun to fire. The announcer called, "Ready," then fired the gun. I released my car and jumped to my feet. "Go car, go," I shouted. I wanted to be first across the finish line, but not today. I was eliminated.

Although I lost, I was excited that my car did so well. During the award ceremony I was sitting in the back waiting for the whole thing to get over, when I heard my name announced. I had won second place in design. The good news was not over yet. When all the awards were given out and we were packing to go home, my advisor came over to tell me that I was given a wild card spot in the state competition. He told me I had a great design and all I needed to do was to get the right gear ratio from motor pulley to drive wheel pulley and I would have a winner. It was the most exciting news of the day. I knew this car could win.

It was back to grandpa's to boost the power. It was a month before the state competition, not much time to get the perfect ratio. I worked on my car every free minute I had. Through trial and error and racing it in the store parking lot against a stop watch, I realized the larger pulley had to be on the motor. It looked like the ratio was three to one. Grandpa found a couple of old tape players and I tore them apart looking for pulleys. I found two pulleys that the ratio between them was three to one.

We tested the car in the workshop using a bright light as the sun. Yes! This was it. Grandpa brought me back down to the parking lot. It was sunny with no wind. Perfect racing conditions. I set up the guide wire and got set to go.

"Are you ready?" Papa said. The big race is this weekend, this had to be it. "Ready, get set, go," Papa hollered. I released my racer and it took off. "Wow," I yelled, "it's gathering speed." "Jessica," Papa called as he looked at his stop watch, "it was the best time ever and good enough to win."

The big day was here, not a cloud in the sky and the sun was bright. The races went off as scheduled. I won all my heats and was on my way to the New England Regional's, in Massachusetts, which was only two weeks away. I did a little minor detail work on my car body. I touched up the paint, checked the pulleys, and made sure it was solid. It was good, it was very good, and I was ready. The time went by fast and before I knew it two weeks had gone by and I was on my way to the New England Regional's.

We had to go in two cars, as there was mom and dad, me and my sister Julia, Papa and Gram and my cousin Adam. He would catch my car after it crossed the finish line so it wouldn't crash. The race was held at the college, using part of their blacktop track. It was mid June and this day was going to be sunny, bright, and extremely hot, especially on the track. Being an all day event mom had packed plenty of lunch and a cooler with cold drinks and plenty of water.

We checked the schedule on the big board and I was in the first heat. I went down to the starting line and got my instructions. Butterflies were back in my stomach as I approached the starting line. There would be five cars to a heat and four cars would be eliminated. I got set, and before I knew it, bang, the gun went off and my car took off and gathered speed. I won my first heat. My heart was pounding, I couldn't believe it; I won my first race!

I looked up to the big board that listed who was racing in what lane and what time. Then I heard someone in the stands asking who was that black wild card and how did they get here. I heard papa tell them, "that's my granddaughter, she's the little blonde girl from Cornish, and watch her smoke." Then it hit me as I read the board, all the names were in red except mine. All the other wild cars had been eliminated. I was racing against state and region champions. I went on to win my next three races. I couldn't believe it; I was in the finals and the only wild card. I drew lane two, and I got ready to go.

I crouched at the starting line and waited. I thought the gun would never go off. Then bang and the race was on. The other four cars had a faster start than mine, but I knew mine would gain speed. At the half way point I passed the car in lane four then went ahead of the car in lane five; only two other cars to pass. I went by the car in lane three and was gaining fast on the car in lane one. We were nearing the finish line and we were neck and neck, then we crossed the finish line. People were standing and applauding, but we still didn't know who won.

There was no instant replay or a camera for a photo finish. The judges at the finish line would determine the winner. Then the announcement came, the winner of the New England Regional was, not me. I finished second, just a fraction of an inch from winning. I got a big trophy and a beautiful plaque for best in design. I was happy, I was the little blonde girl in the seventh grade from the little town of Cornish that beat several champions and finished runner up. I felt great. Thank you Papa; I couldn't have done it without you!

RUDY SAVES THE GOBBLERS

By Eugene Pacetti

The leaves had already turned a bright red, orange and yellow and were now blowing all over the barnyard. It was nippy this evening as the turkeys gathered around the grain troth filling their bellies.

Rudy, the big fat gobbler, and leader, called the turkeys together behind the barn for a big announcement. "OK you all," Rudy said "listen up. Do you know what time of year this is?" Lucy, the blonde turkey, gobbled up and said, "It's close to winter 'cause it's getting cold."

"You're right," said Rudy, "But there's a holiday coming up that's not our favorite, no presents here." Rudy with a lump in his throat gobbled out, "Thanksgiving, that's what coming."

Then all the turkeys hung their heads and gave a low gobble, gobble, gobble as they remembered last year there used to be 7 turkeys in the barnyard. This was the time of the year when one disappeared.

"OK all you birds listen up. We've got to stay hidden 'till after Thanksgiving. Don't eat too much, you don't want to get all fat and plump. And if you see the farmer coming sound a gobble alarm." It was the day before Thanksgiving, early in the morning, when all six turkeys met behind the barn to listen to Rudy's plan. They would slip through the fence and go to the woods. Here they could hide in the leaves and up in the trees. Now they were safe.

The next day was Thanksgiving and the turkeys watched all the family gather for a big feast. The sons and daughters came and nieces and nephews, and this year there were grandchildren. It was late evening when they all finally left. Rudy called the birds together and counted 1, 2, 3, 4, 5, and Rudy was 6. "OK, it's safe to go back to the yard, we've made it through Thanksgiving," Rudy proudly gobbled.

When they got back to the barnyard the troth was full of grain and they all had their fill. It sure was good to get back home, safe.

"Gobble, gobble," said Lucy. "Has anyone seen the PIG??"

MY FIRST BEAR HUNT
By Eugene Pacetti

It was early fall and the air was crisp as bright colored leaves were falling from the trees. Saturday was the first day of bear hunting and it was going to be my first bear hunt. I had turned 16 and my dad had promised me, when I was 16, I could go bear hunting.

I was going with my dad, who had shot three bears, my Uncle Erwin, who had killed two bears, and my Uncle Arthur, who had bagged four.

My dad and his two brothers owned several hundred acres on a mountain in Orange County, Vermont. This was wild country which produced many big bucks along with good hunting for rabbit, partridge, and pheasant. A stream that ran down the mountain provided excellent trout fishing. This mountain was my most favorite place to enjoy nature.

I had helped build a cabin on the mountain. This allowed us to spend the night and be ready to go hunting in the morning. Early on Friday afternoon we packed up our gear and we were off for a week-end of bear hunting.

When we arrived at the cabin we built a fire in the pot belly stove, unpacked our gear then went out to scout for signs of bear. Each had their favorite spot, where they had shot a bear, and they would clean the area and make it comfortable to sit and watch. I was given a spot, which I cleaned, against a big oak tree. As I looked down the hill I could see smoke coming from the chimney.

When we got back to the cabin, my dad took out some bear steaks and said, "When you go hunting for bear, you gotta have a good bear steak. This will make you hunt better, knowing what's going in your belly." After we ate, they told scary stories of bear hunts of the past. How a bear could sneak up on you without being heard and grab you in a bear hug. When a bear stands on his hind legs, opens his mouth and growls it makes the ground shake.

They told me to make the first shot count, 'cause a wounded bear would charge you and claw you to pieces. They told the story of big George, the biggest, meanest bear on the whole mountain. When he raised up on his hind legs he stood over ten feet tall and would weigh in over four hundred pounds. They proceeded to tell me that if I shot a bear I would have to gut it out and I would have to skin it.

I hit the bunk early, with visions of shooting my first bear. Boy I thought, what if I killed Big George. I'd be famous, I'd get my picture in the paper and everyone would want to hear the story of how I shot Big George. I woke up early, it was still dark outside, and I decided to slip out and get to my spot. I wanted to be the first one to shoot a bear. It was a cold morning and I could see my footprints in the heavy frost where I had walked up from the cabin.

I had been sitting against that big oak tree for about twenty minutes when I saw a light in the cabin and smoke curled out the chimney. I wondered if my dad and my two uncles missed me.

My foot was going to sleep, so I decided to stand up and stretch. This might be a good time to look around, I didn't want that big bear to sneak up on me. I heard a little scuffle on the other side of the tree, my heart raced and my body was warm real quick. I thought to myself, it must be a little squirrel and here I am all excited and scared.

I slowly stepped around the tree and all I saw was black, I jumped back, scared was not the word for what I felt. The bear was as surprised as I was, he didn't know I was on the other side of the tree. He raised up on his hind legs and gave the loudest roar I have ever heard. I started to raise my gun and as quick as lighting he swung his paw at me and knocked the gun out of my hands. My mind told my feet to get moving and get us out of here. I turned to run and I remembered what my dad had told me about bears and how they run. "Son," he said, "If you ever have to run from a bear, run down hill. Bears can't run down hill very fast because their front feet are smaller than their hind legs."

The cabin was down hill and I started to run as fast as I could. Was the bear close behind me? Am I going to make it to the cabin? Just as I got to the cabin I looked over my shoulder, that bear was hot on my tail. I reached for the door handle, my toe got caught in a root and I went face first to the ground. The cabin door swung open and that bear ran right over the top of me and into the cabin.

I jumped up, shut the door and hollered, "Skin him guys I'll be back with another one."

SANTA'S LAST STOP

By Jessica Robin Cooper

It started out as your average "Twas the night before Christmas" as Santa headed out to his last stop, the "Little House on the Prairie."

Santa hollers out, "Turn up your light Rudolph this is a dawg gone small roof to land on."

"Gotcha Santa," Rudolph answers, "I'll guide us right in. Slow down for the landing, Dasher."

"You're outta your gord," yelled Dasher, "We can't land on that little roof. Let's use the yard."

Santa shouts, "No way Dasher, that ain't my style. I'm going down that chimney. Ho, ho, ho, slow us down."

Dasher exclaims, "Now Dancer, now Prancer, bring it in hard, Santa will be mad if we fall in the yard."

As the sleigh and the reindeer slid on the snow laden roof, yelling filled the night air.

"Ooooh!" screamed Vixen, "We're going over the edge."

Then Donder replies, "Shut up Vixen, and pull back hard."

"My leg's hanging over the edge," Blitzen blats out.

"Ho, ho, ho," exclaims Santa, "Quit complaining; we made it, didn't we. That old chimney caught us."

Comet acknowledges, "Sure it did; now Donder get your antlers out of my ribs."

"Oh Comet," says Donder, "You're such a wimp."

Jolly ole Santa sings out as he hops out of the sleigh, "Ho, ho, ho, Get ready for the take off boys and girls, I'm going down the chimney and I'll be right back."

"Well if you ask me, you'll never make it Santa," yells Cupid. "It's a small chimney and I don't show it on the list to go down. Toooo small."

"Well I got my bag and I'm on my way," laughed Santa, "Ho, ho, ho, Ugh, ooff Ugh, gimme a little push Comet."

Comet shrugs, "I'm on the take off team, Santa, Vixen you help push."

Vixen grunts, "I can't, ooh, I'm holding Blitzen, he's falling off the roof."

Dasher pops up, "Here's a push, oompa."

"Ho, Ho, Hold it," grunts Santa, "I'm stuck and can't move, Rudolph get me outta here."

"I got the light," says Rudolph, "Prancer can pull."

"Ugh, ooff," Prancer grunting, as he tries to get a better grip.

"You've put on a little weight this year Santa."

"Ouch, let go of my beard, ya dummy," Santa replies.

Donder offers his harness to put around Santa. Once the harness is on Donder yells,

"Dash away, dash away, dash away Dancer.

"Sure," Dancer says, "I got the legs, I gotta do all the work."

Then Santa, in a loud voice, bellows, "OK!!" I'm all set, now pull, pull."

POP, like a cork coming out of a bottle, Santa was free and rolling down the roof. Kathunk he lands in the yard.

"Now that you're in the yard Santa," Rudolph says, "I'll light your way to the front door."

"Bring back some cookies," laughs Cupid.

Vixen was quick to reply, "Oh shut up Cupid, you're overweight now." Then yells, "OK let's set up for the take off. Comet, gets us around the yard."

On comes Rudolph's light as he hollers, "Here he comes, get ready for that 'ol spring to the sleigh and that stupid whistle.

Santa jumps in the sleigh and in a loud groan says, "Get us outta here, move it, move it, I'm tired and I just wanna GO HOME!!"

As they flew out of sight you could hear the reindeer singing, MERRY CHRISTMAS TO ALL AND TO ALL A GOOD NIGHT.

Section Two:

Poems

A NEW YEAR BEGINS

By Eugene Pacetti

The land lies dead beneath a coat of white,
Stillness chills the air at early light.
We feel the strength of winters glow,
As all lay dormant beneath the snow.

The frozen land is not really dead,
But merely lies still as tucked in bed.
Soon heaven's light and warmth will flow,
To bring forth the earth so all will grow.

The sun rises higher and the days grow longer,
As winter fades now spring is stronger.
Earth's white cover will melt and soon disappear,
Colors form from budding flowers will now appear.

Alive with song the birds do sing,
The land is alive and will surely bring,
Sweet, sweet scents from the soft falling dew,
From this land where cold, cold snow was new.

A YEAR PASSES BY

By Eugene Pacetti

A year has passed
A new year now begins
The ground is white with snow
With whistling howling winds.

The next month is the shortest
But the snow remains steadfast.
By the fireside we count the days.
How long will winter last?

March comes in like a lion
With swirling winds that plunder.
Will it leave just like a lamb?
We all begin to wonder

Here come the rains of April
To wash away the snow.
And make the land so fertile,
The flowers now will grow.

May turns the land to a rainbow
With flowers shining bright.
The days keep growing longer,
So now we have more light.

June arrives in all its glory.
Arise the gardens and lawns to mow.
Summer is here, the air is warm.
Get your suit, to the beach we'll go.

Look back to when our land was born.
Patriotism now flies on high.
The red, white and blue we proudly show.
The month we enter is now July.

Dog days of August are upon us.
We count the days since our last rain.
We water the garden so it will grow.
We stay in the shade or get sunburn pain.

The labor force we do salute.
Kids get new clothes for back to school.
The air is changing so we get ready
To button up and close the pool.

Bright colored leaves now fill the air.
Hunters get ready to bring home the meat.
Women in the kitchen now are canning,
For all to have a winter treat.

November brings us into autumn,
When all vegetation seems to die.
Dull are the colors of tan and brown.
Soon upon pure white snow will lie.

Jolly old St. Nick this month will bring,
Many presents for all and spread good cheer.
Good will we show will warm our soul.
Then usher out, this long, long year.

The process now will start again,
With the land covered in a blanket of snow.
As the days sail by one by one.
You'll wonder where this year did go.

MY SNOW MAN

By Eugene Pacetti

Winters in New England bring a lot of snow and children of all ages go out and make snow creatures of all kinds. One day I decided to make myself a big round snow man.

I made myself a snowman,
As perfect as could be.
I thought I'd keep him as a friend
And let him sleep with me.
I made him some pajamas,
And a pillow for his head.
Then that night he ran away,
But first he wet the bed.

MY VALENTINE

By Eugene Pacetti

Is Cupid an angel, Sent from above?
To send an arrow
Through the heart of my love.

How will she know,
That the arrow is mine?
Should I also send her
A Valentine.

Something sweet
Like chocolates I'll send.
To show her my love
Will never end.

Should I ask her out,
To be wined and dined?
Surely with this
True love she will find.

Should I be subtle?
Or must I be bold?
To show her my love,
Will never grow cold.

YOU!

By Jessica Robin Cooper

Soft kiss
On my head
I miss alone in bed.

Hands so warm
A gentle touch
Though I squirm
They're never too much.

A look,
Just one
Is all it took.
I wouldn't turn to run.

Awake at night,
Missing you here,
Holding me tight
With you near.

I'll always be true
And rise above
For you
And your love.

WHAT IS LOVE ?

By Eugene Pacetti

Love is a funny thing,
It's shaped just like lizard.
It wraps itself around your heart,
And nibbles at your gizzard.

Love is found in funny places,
I found it once, behind a little hut.
It was shaped just like a paddle,
And daddy used it on my butt.

Love comes in all shapes and sizes,
It can be a funny looking thing,
That you can not comprehend,
Or it can be that diamond ring.

I'm afraid to say I love you,
For fear you'll say it back,
So I'll say it in the mirror,
Then courage I won't lack.

I LOVE YOU

By Jessica Robin Cooper

Three little words
They mean so much
And with you come so easy,
Just one simple touch.

I look into your eyes,
So honest and true,
You've given me your heart.
So tender and new.

Time has been so little,
But the feeling so great,
The way you look at me I know,
This must be fate.

I wake each day,
Wishing you were here,
I know if it's in His plan,
You will soon be near.

No scale is big enough,
No word is just right,
To describe the way,
I feel when you hold me tight.

I took a chance,
I made the leap,
I saw you there,
And me you can keep.

CUPID'S ARROW

By Eugene Pacetti

There's a chubby little boy
With bow in hand.
When he shoots his arrow,
In your heart it will land.

With wings so small,
How does he fly?
He looks like a fat
Little bird in the sky.

When his arrow hits you,
Love makes you blind.
Where ever she is
True love you will find.

She may have pimples,
Or muscles galore.
But it's only her
That you will adore.

You'll bring her roses,
And a box of chocolate,
And a picture of you
Stuck in a locket.

She'll give you her love,
And call you sweet thing.
You know what she wants,
On her finger a ring.

Now wedding bells chime,
As you walk down the aisle.
Soon three on your form,
For taxes you'll file.

WITH A BLINK OF AN EYE

By Eugene Pacetti

Winter's gone
The rain has come
No more snow
Here come the sun.

Spring has sprung
The grass has riz
I wonder where
The flowers is.

Come on Summer
Get here soon.
I'll go to the beach
And dig with my spoon.

Then comes the Fall.
Now Summer's gone.
All the leaves in the trees,
Are now on the lawn.

Look at the snow
Now winter's here
I'll sit by the fire,
And sip on my beer.

Wow, look out the window,
Snow's melting now.
Spring's finally here.
But I don't know how.

Seasons go by,
With the wink of an eye.
Summer slips in,
Then slides right by.

A HERO NAMED MOM

By Jessica Robin Cooper

When I'm batting zero,
My Mom is my hero.

She doesn't drape a cape,
From the back of her nape.

She carries a grin,
Just above her chin.

When I'm low and wear a frown,
She picks me up from way, way down.

Some times mom's outrageous,
But she always acts courageous.

When really at heart,
We are never apart.

Mom doesn't mean made of money,
She always greets me with, "Hi honey.

Moms must come from way above,
"Cause they're always giving lots of love.

WHAT MOM DID FOR ME

By Eugene Pacetti

Never forget what your mom did for you all through your life.

Who held me tight to her breast when I was born?
Who cuddled me up and kept me warm?
Who dried my butt and powered me up and put on sweet smelly stuff?
Who watched me crawl and laughed at the way I got around?
Who's arms were out stretched when I took my first step?
Who rubbed my gums with paregoric when my first tooth was trying to come out?
Who was my nurse when I was sick and understood all my little hurts?
Who shed a tear when I was left at school on that first day?
Who bought me an ice cream cone when I was good?
Who put me in time out when I was naughty?
Who helped me with my homework and guided me through school?
Who cried when I graduated, because she was so proud?
Who cried again when I went off to college?
Who harped on me to do good, then told me how proud she was of me when I did good?
Who was crying again when I got married?
Now I've got a family of my own and I know how she feels.
My kids call her grandma, nana or noni.
I call her MOM.
May all the mothers in the world have a great Mother's Day what ever stage you're going through.
And God bless you grandmothers who have been through all these stages and now are doing it again.
HAPPY MOTHER'S DAY

MY DAD

By Eugene Pacetti

Kids have been bragging about their Dads for years and years. They tell how good their Dad is and how strong he is. Dad can do many great things. Let's go back in time and hear what some kids said a long, long time ago

My Dad picked up his sword and slew the mighty dragon.
My Dad picked up his sling and took down the giant Goliath.
My Dad was baptized by Mosses.
My Dad walked with Jesus.
My Dad was an architect that designed the great pyramids.
My Dad planned the great wall of China.
My Dad sailed the ship that landed in America.
My Dad was the first to land on Plymouth Rock.
My Dad blazed a trail across the wilderness.
My Dad drove a wagon train across America.
My Dad found gold in California.
My Dad fought for liberty, to keep our nation one.
My Dad fought for our civil rights.
My Dad went across the sea to fight in a big world war.
My Dad invented medicines that would cure the sick.
My Dad built and airplane, now all the world can fly.
My Dad played baseball with Babe Ruth.
My Dad played football for Vince Lombardi.
What did you say about your Dad?
I'll bet we've all done a little bragging about Dad.
On Father's Day just tell him what a great Dad he is.

THE MAN I MARRIED

By Jessica Robin Cooper

It's just too much,
The heartbreak.
Almost unbearable,
But time is what I'll take.

Close my eyes,
Trust in him,
He knows my path,
His will, not a whim.

Protect my heart,
Time to heal.
Two hands together,
I now kneel.

He introduced me to you,
After some time did pass,
Lightening my heart,
With your humor and sass.

Precious as a gem,
To you I'm like gold,
Treating me wonderfully,
As you were raised and told.

Brick by brick,
Day by day,
You opened my heart,
As I did pray.

A kiss so soft,
A touch so gentle,
A look so caring,
And a heartbeat so instrumental.

We have begun,
Hand in hand,
A journey in life,
Feelings we understand.

When I least expected,
He answered my prayer.
I turned around,
And you were there.

OUR GOLDEN ANNIVERSARY

By Eugene Pacetti

It was our 50th anniversary and I wrote a special poem about our life together. We were both retied and had moved to Chapel Hill, TN where my wife grew up. Except for our vacation time, when we went to Chapel Hill to visit her family, she had been away from home for almost 50 years. Her love for me and our family had kept her away from her siblings. We went to church and Sunday school at Smyrna Baptist, where she was baptized and went to as a child.

I, being from Vermont, found myself making a new home in the deep south. Would I be accepted in her church? Would I fit in with her friends? I quickly learned the answer would be YES. I wrote this poem to tell her my love was true, and to tell the Sunday school class thank you for accepting me. On our 50th anniversary I read this to the Adult 4 Sunday school class.

It was 50 years ago,
I took myself a wife.
We sailed life's sea together,
And she brightened up my life.

We thought the sea was smooth,
When we started life together.
Never thought that some day
We would face some stormy weather.

One thing was in our favor,
When we stood and truly vowed.
That God was at the helm,
To crash was not allowed.

God blessed us three times,
Called them David, Karen and Mike.

They are all so beautiful,
And they're not at all alike.

They grew so fast,
And now have lives of their own.
They've given us nine grandchildren,
And a great grandson that stands alone.

Many friends we've had through out the years,
Many miles we did travel.
The roads all led to here,
Our stories to unravel.

Through all our life,
Two blessings we truly got from God.
Best know as friends and family.
To Him we now applaud.

With friends like you we are truly blessed,
We thank you from our heart.
Our roots now planted here,
We hope to never part

OUR THANKSGIVING TURKEY

By Eugene Pacetti

It was getting close to Thanksgiving, and we all wondered,
Would dad kill the old turkey, or would he blunder.
The gobbler did strut through the barn yard with pride.
And my sister confessed the big axe she did hide.
Our dad was quite when he went to the shed.
He quickly returned, took his hat off his head.
Spun around once and threw his hat to the floor.
With a scowl looked at mom and he said, "I am sore."
Mom tried to console him, and said, "Tell me dear,
What happened to you, what's your greatest fear?"
"That old bird I've fattened for our Thanksgiving treat,
If I don't find my axe, we'll have nothing to eat."
"My dear what I'll do is add veggies to the plate,
I'll bake more pies, it's not too late."
"That old bird, as he struts in the yard, with each gobble he mocks me."
"After Thanksgiving the neighbors come 'round, everyone will surely see."
"That I lack the courage to kill the old bird,
And others will tell of the coward they heard."
I had an idea; I called my sister and brother Ted.
We went upstairs and got under the bed.
Broke open my piggy bank to get the money inside.
Is there enough for a turkey so plump and wide?
To the store we did rush with money in hand.
Then asked the grocer, "Can we get a turkey as big as we planned?"
He smiled, then laughed as his belly shook.
Then he took a big bird off the cooler room hook.
All the way home we really did fly.
Would we be too late? Would the old turkey die?
Dad stood in the doorway, with turkey in arm.
In his hand was a butcher knife. This was cause for alarm.

"No dad, please don't, look what we got."
"A fat turkey for dinner with our pennies we bought."
The old bird got excited, and flew out to the yard.
Dad turned, looked at us, and his stare was hard.
Then a smile broke through, and his laugh was a roar.
"I couldn't kill that old bird; I was going to the store."
"I called the butcher to save us a bird."
"Then he called me back, said you kids gave him the word."
Now we'll have a fat turkey and all will survive.
Happy Thanksgiving, our gobbler's alive.

TIME TO BE THANKFUL

By Eugene Pacetti

It was years ago when I was working as a teacher's assistant. Thanksgiving was getting close and the students were anxiously getting ready for the up coming holiday. We talked about what we were going to have for our big Thanksgiving feast. Turkey was the main course, with potato and gravy. No one got excited over the vegetables. Then I asked the students what they were thankful for this year. I got a wonderful response and wrote this poem based on their thoughts.

The children all are thankful
For the school that they attend.
And for the caring teachers,
And the lessons that they send.

Each student has a thought,
Of what they're thankful for.
Expressions brought to light,
Show they care even more.

Gerald is thankful for Mr. P.
He makes the learning fun,
In the electricity course.
Gerald makes his circuit run.

Wanda taps her foot to tunes,
Soft music we must keep.
She's thankful for the stereo
And the bean bag with the sheep.

Albert loves computers and puzzles,
And it's fun just making a friend.
He's thankful for all the teachers,
And the hands to him they lend.

Alex likes a dinosaur,
He likes Hulk Hogan too.
But he's really, really thankful,
For that old horse, C.W.

Brenden is new to our school,
And he fits in very nice.
He's thankful for a lot of things
A great sister, she's cool as ice.

Bubba is a lovable bear,
In school he's never bad.
He loves and is so thankful,
For his granddaddy Brad.

Jimmy has a great big smile,
He likes to look real sharp.
He's so thankful for all those shirts,
That makes him look the part.

Pete's family means a lot to him,
And to have a friend like Jent.
For those he's truly thankful,
For the love that they have spent.

Les is happy and go lucky,
And he never gets real sore.
He's thankful for ole Barney,
And he loves that dinosaur.

Joe yells through his megaphone,
And cheers his team ahead.
He's thankful for those cheerleaders,
That makes his face turn red.

Shelia's a tiny sweetheart,
And can not reach the net.
Now she's really thankful,
For that shorter goal – you bet.

Lori's a lovable little girl,
Teachers say she's like a dove.
She's thankful for her family,
That taught her how to love.

Now take time to reflect,
On all these students fine.
Now aren't you truly thankful,
They love you all the time.

WHAT I DID TODAY

By Eugene Pacetti

I shed a little tear today,
For someone that I love.
For they may be gone tomorrow,
Fly away just like a dove.

I gave a little smile today,
To someone feeling sad.
I tried to cheer them up,
For no one should be mad.

I gave a little hug today,
To someone very dear.
I told them that I loved them,
And would always keep them near.

I shook the hand of a stranger today,
And introduced myself to him.
I said, "You know God loves you."
He said, "Do you think his love will win?"

I got a phone call today,
From a friend I've know for years.
He told me that his wife just died,
For him I shed my tears.

A wonderful group I met today,
They do God's work and travel.
To those in need they give their help,
So God's love will not unravel.

As you go about your life today,
Touch someone's life with meaning.
Show God's love to all you meet,
In your face it'll show with beaming.

THIS RULER

By Eugene Pacetti

When I was working as a Teacher Assistant, the teacher had to have a serious operation. She was out of school for two months. When she returned we had a little welcome back party with the students. I had a ruler that unfolded to six feet, and as I read this poem I would unfold part of the ruler. At the end of the poem I opened it up completely.

If this ruler would stretch across the state,
That's how much we need you,
The kids can hardly wait.

If this ruler would reach across the land,
That's how much we care for you,
We'll all strike up the band.

If this ruler would go around the world,
This is how much you're appreciated,
Our banners are unfurled.

If this ruler would make it to the stars,
That's how much we love you,
From the bottom of our hearts.

Tears came to her eyes and she gave everyone a big hug.

WHAT IS JESSICA?

By Laurie Fairall Head

While at the University of Tennessee, I co-oped at the city of Maryville.
When I left, my friend Laurie wrote this to me. Little did we know, when
I graduated, I'd be back to Maryville.

A young lady so sweet
It's always a pleasure to greet

She has a bright cheerful smile
She's someone who goes the extra mile.

She is a steadfast and true friend,
Through the good and the bad times, right 'till the end.

She's thoughtful, considerate and kind,
Talented and skilled with a strong intelligent mind.

Natural blonde with eyes so pretty and blue,
For some special man, she'll give her love true.

Her future is bright,
With endless options in sight.

She will be greatly missed here at work,
Especially all of her funny little quirks!

Best wishes always
Laurie Fairall

I'LL NEVER LEAVE YOU

By Eugene Pacetti

This is a poem from me to my family. I hope someone will read it after I've gone and remember how much I love every one of you. My love for all of you will shine down from heaven. Take care of mom; they don't come any better than gram.

What are you doing there?
Do I see a falling tear?
I will never leave you,
I'll always be right here

Take a minute to stop and think,
Of all the good times we have had.
I'm sure you all remember them.
I know it's hard, but don't be sad.

There are pictures you can share
Of the good times we had together.
Tell all the little ones about me,
We knew it wouldn't be forever.

I loved you all so very much,
I hope I taught you well.
I've tried to be a Christian true,
So I won't go to hell.

I left a lot of stuff,
For all of you to share.
Some of it you gave me,
Because you really care.

I hope I'm leaving memories,
That will bring a loving smile.
You all have been a joy to me,
That made my life worthwhile.

When ever you have a question,
Along life's traveled way,
Take a moment and ask yourself,
What would I have to say?

And as you go through life,
Trying with all your might,
To keep your ship a sail,
Through a dark and stormy night.

Think of me and the love we shared,
I'll calm the storm and ease your mind,
And bring you safely home,
For you see, I'm in your heart you'll find.

Now let's dry those tears,
And hug each one for me.
It's a short trip to heaven,
Some day you all will see.

Look up into the sky at night,
You see that twinkling star,
That's me; I'm winking back at you.
You see, I'm not so very far.

When you've done all your home work,
And an A is placed upon your test,
Remember it was me that told you,
To always do your best.

Well I got to go now,
But never have a fear,
Just call me if you need me.
I'll always be right here.

A SOLDIER DIES

By Eugene Pacetti

A soldier's death is a tragedy of war. How many son and daughters must die to preserve peace on earth? How many fathers and mothers will not see their children grow up?

A red rose lay upon the grave,
For him who gave his life today.
He fought with valor and with honor,
So we may go to church and pray.

We're free to take our chosen path,
To live our life as we desire.
He died so far away from home,
With courage and bravery we all admire.

Not long ago in mother's arms,
He was a babe that needed love.
Then a man he soon became,
Now God has taken him up above.

How much blood must be shed,
For the world to live in peace?
How much anger, fear, and hatred,
Must all the world release?

WHEN I WAS YOUNG

By Eugene Pacetti

When I was young,
And went to school,
I studied hard,
Learned the golden rule.

Now I'm old,
In school I teach
Those special kids
I try to reach.

When I was young,
And in my prime,
I'd go fishing
Any old time.

Now I'm old,
My legs do squeak,
Haven't been fishing,
In over a week.

When I was young,
I'd hunt some deer.
And a trophy buck,
I shot one year.

Now I'm old,
The game I see,
Is when I watch
Dis cov er ee.

When I was young,
The girls they came,
To watch me play
In a football game.

Now I'm old,
Got a bad back,
Can't let the girls,
See me take a sack.

When I was young,
It was party time.
Stayed out all night,
And I felt fine.

Now I'm old,
I party slow,
When the clock hits ten,
Off to bed I go.

When I was young,
This beauty I see,
And said to her
"Will you marry me?"

Now I'm old,
She's a beauty so fair.
All I can say is,
I'm loosing my hair.

When I was young,
My wife was great,
She could cook,
And I'd clean my plate.

Now I'm old,
She still looks great.
But look at me,
Still gaining weight.

When I was young,
Cars didn't go fast,
They were built to serve,
And made to last.

Now I'm old,
Speed is the rule,
If I drove like that,
I'd be a dead fool.

When I was young,
And I turned thirty,
To think about forty,
Was something dirty.

Now I'm old,
I'm reflecting on time,
Today I just turned
To a young sixty-nine.

GETTING DRESSED TO GO OUT

By Eugene Pacetti

Some of you men can relate to this. You just can't seem to pick the right clothes to wear if you're out some where, with your wife.

As I started to get dressed,
And I took out my clothes,
A voice rang out loud and clear,
"Honey, you are not wearing those."

I thought my choice was good,
I wore them the day before.
Wearing them again would save washing.
I guess these points I didn't score.

That clear voice rang out again,
You wore those yesterday,
They now go in the laundry.
To wear them tonight I must say nay.

Here you go, put these on,
The socks I leave your choice.
So I got dressed and ready to go,
Not wanting to hear that loud clear voice.

So look at me now, boy I look good,
But I can't take the credit,
My wife picked the clothes,
For my pick of duds is just a bad habit.

SUMMER IS HERE
By Eugene Pacetti

It's near the end of May and the kids are getting antsy and can't wait to get out of school. Here's a short poem about how One student feels as he sits in class on the last day of school.

As I sit and look out the window,
My school work's all done now.
Waiting for the bell to ring,
To tell me school's out—WOW.

June brings on the summer,
As the earth produces vegetation,
And the land brings forth life,
Without the slightest hesitation.

Beaches are alive with surfers,
Bathers absorb the summer sun.
Sailboats cruise along the horizon,
No other season brings on such fun.

The long days of summer will pass to soon,
Feel the air, now it's turning cool.
Where shall we go, what path to take?
Then here we are; we're back in school.

Section Three:

Religious

HOW THE WORLD BEGAN

By Eugene Pacetti

Scientists have a logical explanation on how the world began, but they left out a small three letter word with a big meaning, GOD. This is my personal view on the beginning of earth and the universe.

Our earth began thousands of millions of years ago as part of God's plan. God placed a vast cloud of dust and gasses in what is now our solar system.

In the course of millions of years, God created gravity in the center of this cloud. (You must remember that as we measure time in millions of years, this is only a short period of time for God.) This gravity caused the cloud to collapse into a flat disc. Rotating around its center, gravity drew the heavy materials toward the center. This was to become the sun.

The lighter materials surrounding the central core broke into huge rings around the sun. These rings became our earth and other planets in a dense cold darkness. God saw the darkness and cold were not good, so he created heat and light.

Over a period of millions of years, God created a nuclear reaction allowing the sun cloud to shrink. With the passing of millions of years the sun became a glowing mass of ever burning gasses. Today this gives us light and heat.

Millions of years later, as part of God's plan, the rings of gas and dust formed into flaming balls and became planets. Our earth was about 2,000 times its present size and was hot and solid. God formed the earth like a ball of putty. Then He let it harden to form a thin covering. As the earth cooled it shrank, and as the earth shrank it created mountains. The cooling continued for millions of years and the cooling continues today.

The earth was now being pounded by rocks that created hollows and craters, while under the earth's crust there was still molten lava. Through millions of years, while the earth was cooling, clouds of dust gasses were pouring out of the cracks. These gasses were being held close to earth by gravity.

God saw the earth was hard and hot, and as the lower clouds

blanketed the earth they turned to water. God said let there be rain, and the rains beat upon the earth. Millions of years passed and water formed on earth. As the rain drops pelted the earth, the surface crumbled to dirt and the depression flowed with water and became rivers and the crater became oceans, seas and lakes.

As millions of years went by, the earth continued to change and God watched. Earthquakes and volcanic eruptions destroyed large mountains and created new ones. Beds in the seas were raise and became continents. God surveyed the earth and saw this was good.

Then God swept away the cloud that covered the sun, and earth was with light and heat. Then God separated the light into night and day and said this is good.

God looked at the earth and decided it needed life to enjoy what he had created, so he created the simplest form of life we call a protoplasm, which is the basis of all living things. Over millions of years the protoplasm developed into complete cells. God watched his life forms develop into living things of many cells and said, "This is good."

Millions of years went by and the seas were creating all types of life forms. God saw the land was barren and it also needed plant life forms. God swept the cell life from the sea and floated them onto the land and they produced what we know as chlorophyll. From these cells grew plants.

For millions of years the rains turned rock to dust which became soil to allow the plants to grow. The plants flourished and large trees began to grow, and God saw this was good.

As time went by and the rains let up, some of the water on the land dried up, so God made it possible for the sea creatures to live on land by giving them lungs to breathe air. The earth became rich with vegetation and was suitable for life and God said, "This is good."

THIS EASTER SEASON

By Eugene Pacetti

If peace came to the world,
I can give you the reason,
Christ rose from the dead.
This Easter season.

But wars were not taken away,
The day Christ came alive.
He died for our sins,
So we all would survive.

How we live our lives,
God gives us a choice,
To sin and be quiet,
Or ask forgiveness, with our voice.

Tell God that you love Him,
His son did not die in vain.
Prayer can reach God,
And help sooth your pain.

Would you give up your son,
To save the world's sinners?
For your son, is the war over?
Are we really the winners?

The best we can do now,
To the Lord go in prayer.
Thank you God for your son,
Was his death really fair?

Christ rising from the dead,
Today we applaud.
For now Jesus sits,
At the right hand of God.

THE RESURRECTION

By Eugene Pacetti

This is the season
We all rejoice,
For Christ has risen,
As this was God's choice

We must not forget the events that led to this great celebration.

Christ told Peter, "Before the cock crows, you will deny me thrice."

Pilate asked the crowd, "What am I to do with Jesus, who is called Christ." The crowd yelled, "Let him be crucified."

Pilate washed his hands saying, "I am innocent of the blood of this just man."

Pilate released Christ to Barabbas.

The soldiers took Jesus into the praetorium, stripped him and put on him a scarlet cloak; and plaiting a crown of thorn, they put it upon his head.

They mocked him saying, "Hail, king of the Jews."

They put his own garments back on and led him to be crucified.

And with the cross he carried, Christ also carried the sins of us all.

Spikes were driven into his hands and feet as he hung there to die.

As life was leaving his body, He looked to the heaven and said, "Forgive them Father for they know not what they do."

With the glory of the resurrection, we must not forget the suffering.

HALLELUJAH

By Eugene Pacetti

Hallelujah, the Lord has risen.
He died on the cross our sins to forgive.
Now alive, he leads us to the father.
He shows us the way we all should live.

Death on the cross
And a dark cold cave
Could not hold our Savior
From our souls to save.

Crucified, all thought he died,
But on day three he did arise.
Christ took our sins away,
And going to heaven would be our prize.

Fall on your knees,
Give thanks to God.
He gave up his son,
For this we applaud.

Thank you God,
Thank you Lord,
Now a river of sins,
I will not ford.

THE SEASONS OF GOD

By Eugene Pacetti

'Tis Fall the air is crisp
The leaves are colored bright.
The artist's hand is God
How they glimmer in the light.

Soon the leaves will fall.
Bare arms reach toward the sky,
As if to say we thank you, God.
Now they appear to die.

A blanket of snow will cover the land.
And the earth entombed will lay,
To await God's shining sun,
And the land will rise this day.

As Christ was dead,
And entombed in a hole.
Truly God's son arose
To cleanse our sinful soul.

The sun will come to warm the earth.
Life will rise through out the land.
Flowers and trees, they all will bloom
By the gardener we know, God's hand.

When all the fruit is harvested,
The cold will be our test.
When the cycle is complete,
The earth will lie and rest.

God cares for us as he does the earth.
He lets us grow to our own will.
What type of harvest will you reap?
Lost crop, or with God your heart to fill.

SUNDAY SCHOOL CLASS
By Eugene Pacetti

I went to Smyrna Baptist Church with my wife and we also attended their Sunday school class. I had a captive audience when I wrote and read my poems and articles. This is a poem I wrote about the members of this Sunday school class.

There's a group that I belong to,
They're kinda old but cool.
A rowdy bunch to say the least,
They use the bible as their tool.

They love to eat and some play golf.
They're always having fun.
Do gooders, yes they are,
They know each day God lifts the sun.

They have a leader, they call him Joe,
Sometimes he gets emotional.
He'll loose his place and blow his nose,
But his classes are sensational.

Joe has a side kick that helps him out.
She knows the Bible better than the rest.
On verses and knowledge, Donna is not short,
When Joe's not there, she'll pass the test.

Some in the group like to sing, But Ellis is the one we hear.
His voice rings out above the rest,
God's words are sweetness to our ear.

This group meets every Sunday morn,
To read and study God's loving plan.
Lewis always gets things started,
When he checks the health of those he can.

There are two sisters in the group,
One's lived here all her days.
The other's back from way up north.
Guess who always gets her ways.
Sadie's words of wisdom,
Are posted on the board.
The words she brings each week,
Are directly from the Lord.

Dot's just gotta leave,
That job of her's behind.
She misses all the outings,
From the store she can't unwind.

Evie watches all our money,
A trustful soul is she.
Sometimes she gets locked out,
But Joe will set her free.

And there's a guy from Texas,
Who's tallest in the group.
You gotta check his feet,
And see those crazy boots.

A golfer in this playful bunch,
Lives on the greens I've heard.
We've never seen his score card.
I think his name is Byrd.

May God bless Earlene,
We pray for her each week.
The group has love and shares it,
As a cure for her we seek.

If you ever want to diet,
Then everyone can learn,
From the thin one in the group,
We call her tiny Burns.

There are many good cooks in this bunch,
Too many to really mention,
But the goodies by McCool,
Will surely get your attention.

Faye sits on the back porch,
Mosquitoes she does swat.
Some day she'll have a screen,
And that will help a lot.

Henson teaches his own class,
He learned his stuff from us.
I think Mary Margaret still takes notes,
So Norman will never fuss.

Helen's right on time,
We must have started early.
She comes in with a great big smile,
Some times I think she's squirrely

If the old man's playing golf,
Pat's with that baby girl.
She surely is a blessing,
That little one's a pearl.

Robert is the quiet one,
Not tall nor dark or handsome.
Just steadfast and always steady,
Every Sunday he will come.

Carlton is the sharp one,
He dresses really neat.
Joyce must pick his clothes out,
You know she's really sweet.

Teeny's not tiny by any means,
She's a sweetheart through and through.
Her heart's the biggest you've ever seen,
She'll give her love to you.

Kenneth's new to the group,
He can't be very old.
I think he's still a puppy,
If the truth were ever told.

I think Shirley should be a teacher,
She has that intelligent look.
Be careful what you say to her,
She'll make you read the good book.

Marie is truly dainty,
Her voice is soft and sweet.
When you get to meet her,
You'll see she's really neat.

Billy thinks that he can sing,
He warbles out the note.
Sometimes I really think,
It gets stuck in his throat.

Carol's a friend to everyone,
Her blessings, they stand tall.
If you ever need to be wanted,
Just give this girl a call.

God has blessed Linda,
With a joyful laugh and smile.
She brightens up this group,
With her pure and happy style.

Our prayers go out to Barbara,
Her courage takes a stand.
She's always there when needed,
With a loving, helping hand.

Hazel is the light in the dark,
She'll help you find your way.
A friend to all she meets,
What more is there to say?

Bruce is the biggest in the group,
He's from Paul Bunyan's family tree.
There's a reason for his size,
For his heart must fit, you see.

The smallest in the group is Clara,
The unfortunate have her love.
With care and understanding,
She stands a head above.

Now did I mention Polly?
A relative of mine.
She's always doing something good,
I really think she's fine.

Oh boy, now there's Frances,
My wife of many years.
I gotta say something sweet,
Or from me she'll draw some tears.

Now comes Eugene, that's me,
I've finally reached the end.
May God bless every one of you,
From me your faithful friend.

Smyrna Baptist Church,
Adult group number four.
The best of all the Sunday schools,
I need not say any more.

AMEN

HOW GOD MADE WOMAN

By Eugene Pacetti

When God made man he blew his breath into some dirt and man was formed. God saw what he had made and He was pleased. The days past and God said, "It is not good for man to be alone, he needs a companion." Then God created woman. When God created woman he took his time, for He needed a creature with intelligence, patients, strength, and agility. She must be stern, but with a lovable personality. God encased this creature so she was beautiful in man's eye. The woman's traits must be precise and balanced for one day a woman would bear his son, Jesus. This is how God made woman

From Adam's rib,
God took a bone,
Created strength,
For her alone.

God molded her,
To have ability,
With movements graceful,
He called agility.

A cup of fortitude,
God put in the blend,
To give her strength of will,
For she must not bend.

He sprinkled her with angel dust,
For patients she will need,
To raise her many children,
Their voices she must heed.

She must be seen by all,
With a lovable personality,
Her skin will be fair,
Her beauty is in simplicity.

She will teach her young,
And raise them strong,
So the world will know,
She can do no wrong.

Man will love and honor her,
And take her for his wife,
He will care and protect her,
All through their earthly life.

When her life on earth is over,
She will take on other chores,
God will see that His creation,
Will open heaven's doors.

I COME TO YOU LORD

By Eugene Pacetti

I come to you, Lord, when I'm troubled,
I seek your help when I'm sad,
I seem to always ask for something,
And use your name in vain, when I'm mad.

I need to ask for your forgiveness,
I need to thank you for all you've done,
I need to pray and think of others,
And to thank you, Lord, for giving your son.

Life has no meaning without you in my heart,
Without the Bible, what path would I follow?
My soul would be empty,
Through life I would wallow.

MY PRAYER FOR YOU

By Eugene Pacetti

PRAYER: n. obtain by begging. The act of asking for a favor with earnestness; a petition, supplication, entreaty; that which is asked; a solemn petition addressed to an object of worship; the words of a supplication; that part of a petition to a public body which specifies the thing desired to be done or granted. Did you ever think that "PRAYER" had such a complicated definition? All this time I thought PRAYER was my conversation with God. Let me give you an example. When I wake up in the morning, I say in my mind, "Thank you God, I sure will enjoy this wonderful day." On Sunday morning I jokingly say to God, "See you in church."
This is my prayer for you.

I said a prayer for you today and know God must have heard.
I felt the answer in my heart, although He spoke no word.
I didn't ask for wealth or fame.
I knew you wouldn't mind.
I asked him to send treasures of a far more lasting kind.
I asked that he be near you at the start of each new day.
To grant you health and blessings and friends to share your way.
I asked for happiness for you in all things great and small.
But it was for his loving care I prayed the most of all.

THE PASTOR WE LOVE

By Eugene Pacetti

This is a poem I wrote for a lady in our church. He was the pastor for her youth group and brought her to Christ.

There was this boy,
That lived on a farm,
Who preached to the cows,
Behind the big barn.

He was given a sign,
To spread the good word,
Both steadfast and strong,
God's message was heard.

To the youth in his church,
An impression he made,
To last for a life time,
That would never fade.

The Holy Spirit,
Came into our heart,
Kept us close to God,
And never apart.

He believed in the youth,
As his music foretold,
Stay young at heart,
We must never grow old.

If we strayed from the path,
And sometimes we fell,
He said God loved us,
We would not go to hell.

He picked us back up,
And showed us the light,
That Christ was the way,
We must stand up and fight.

Remember these places?
Burger King, Dairy Queen,
On Sunday after church,
Did we create a scene?

I think of the rap sessions,
We had Friday nights,
We laughed, cried, and worshipped,
With God in our sights.

As I grew older,
From God I strayed,
Would my sins be forgiven,
If on my knees I prayed?

You came to my aid,
And we prayed on the phone,
Though miles apart,
I was never alone.

Because of you,
God's back in my life,
He'll love me and guide me,
Through all of my strife.

Oh the world, is in such a mess,
And you can't save them all,
But the youth that you loved,
Will surely not fall.

The world needs more,
Preachers with a shaker,
That will lead us to Christ,
Like Winston "GO" Baker.

THE TEST

By Eugene Pacetti

When I go through the day,
With the Lord by my side,
My spirit is lifted,
I have nothing to hide.

No matter what the weather,
It's always sunny and bright,
For the Lord walks with me,
Through the day and all night.

My spirits are all joyful,
Love flows from my heart,
For the Lord has blessed me,
From Him I'll never part.

All through your earthly life,
You'll be blessed by the Lord,
For when you do His bidding,
Many streams you will not ford.

Will you try this tomorrow?
When you first start your day,
Ask the Lord to be with you,
And come travel your way.

You'll feel the powerful surge,
That Christ puts in your soul,
Then you know that His love,
Will have to be told.

When at the end of the day,
You lie down to rest,
You'll feel good just knowing,
The Lord put you to the test.

MY BIBLE

By Eugene Pacetti

The Bible is like a map to heaven,
The directions are written very clear,
No other words are published,
That can bring you even near.

The scriptures foretell of the night,
God sent his only son,
To be born in a lowly manger,
To be worshipped by everyone.

Jesus traveled and healed the sick,
Many miracles He did perform,
He spoke of God in heaven,
And how we'd be reborn.

Our sins His son would now remove,
When on the cross He'd die,
Then in a closed dark tomb,
His body then would lie.

Now three days would pass,
The stone had rolled away,
They searched, the tomb was empty,
For Christ arose this day.

The Bible clearly guides us,
Along the perfect path,
With Christ as our leader,
We must still fear God's wrath.

The Ten Commandments, clearly written,
For everyone to follow,
Then life would be God pleasing,
In sin we would not wallow.

A caring and forgiving God,
The same He loves us all,
The scriptures tell us why,
From His grace we must not fall.

Many times this book was published,
Rewritten for the world claim,
The truth no matter how it's written,
Will always be the same.

Don't be shy or be alarmed,
When you must stand and say,
Thank you Lord,
For now it is my judgment day.

With bible tight in hand,
This last trip you will take,
Through Christ, our Lord,
Our God will not forsake.

Now open this book,
God's word in your palm,
And slowly read,
The 23rd psalm.

The Lord is my shepherd, I shall not want. He maketh me to lie down in green pastures, he leadeth me beside the still waters, He restoreth my soul. He leadeth me in paths of righteousness for His name's sake. Yea though I walk through the valley of the shadow of death, I will fear no evil, for thou art with me; thy rod and thy staff, they comfort. Thou preparest a table before me in the presence of my enemies.

Thou anointest my head with oil; my cup runneth over. Surely goodness and mercy shall follow me all the days of my life: and I will dwell in the house of the Lord forever.

LORD SHOULD I FORGET TO PRAY

By Eugene Pacetti

We all need prayer in our lives. We need someone to talk to that is bigger, stronger, has compassion, and has the power to forgive us. God is all we need.

Lord, if ever I should forget to pray,
For the ones I love on any day.

My forgetfulness please forgive,
As every day for you I live.

Be with me Lord in all I do,
Help me walk closer to you.

Thank you Lord for hearing my prayer,
And thank you Lord for all your care.

Lord, if I should slip and I may fall,
Please pick me up and walk me tall.

The things I do, each day I live,
Good deeds should I most freely give.

To us your son you freely gave,
He died, then rose, our sins to save.

As I look about at your creation,
I thank you Lord for our salvation.

When it comes time to leave this land,
I pray I deserve to hold your hand.

THIS LIFE OF MINE

By Eugene Pacetti

Is this all I have,
This life of mine,
Is there nothing more,
Must I be divine?

What will happen when I die?
I'm truly not with out sin,
When my body lies and decays away,
What will happen to my soul within?

I pray for those who needs God's grace,
In faith I know that I am strong,
Who will be there when I drift away?
To find the place where my soul belongs.

I put my trust in God alone,
For His son died to prepare the way,
When my day comes, I'm not really dead,
My soul lives on to a better day.

I DON'T READ MY BIBLE

By Eugene Pacetti

Do you read your bible every day? Do you read it once a week? Do you read it once in a while? How often do you really read the Bible?

I don't read my Bible,
I know I really should,
There's so much to do,
I'd read if I really could.

I don't read my Bible,
It sets there on the shelf,
I've got to try and read it,
I'll start tomorrow I tell myself.

I don't read my Bible,
There's no time during the day,
I rush about and go to work,
Then take the kids to play.

I don't read my Bible,
I must hear the news report,
By evening I'm too tired,
Or I've got to watch my sport.

Start to read your Bible,
God's words will make you strong,
The books become astounding,
And may keep you from doing wrong.

WHAT DO YOU WEAR WHEN YOU GO TO HEAVEN

By Eugene Pacetti

A few days after a small boy saw his grandfather laid to rest in a new blue suit with gold buttons, he asked his mom,

"Hey mom, did grandpa go to heaven?"
"Yes son, I'm sure that's where he's gone,
"Did he wear his new blue suit,
The one with the gold buttons on?"

"I'm sure that's what he wore,
So he'd look his Sunday best,
When he stood in front of God,
To meet his sternest test."

"What should I wear when I go to heaven?"
I want God to know just where I'm at."
"I know, I'll wear my baseball suit."
"Mom, can I bring my Louisville Slugger bat?"

What will you wear when you go to heaven?
Be sure to wear a smile for all the good you've done,
And hold your head up high,
"Cause heaven will be fun.

You can wear your overalls,
Show God you're a farmer proud,
Many crops you've grown through out the years,
And fed a mighty crowd.

You can wear your football jersey,
As a pro you did your very best,
An example for all the kids you set,
When in heaven, you'll get a rest.

God will know you by what you wear,
You've worn it all your life,
Through all the years of good times,
And how you handled strife.

You can wear the finest makeup,
And put your hair in curls,
But, when you go to heaven,
Your soul to God unfurls.

If you're a knight in shining armor,
And your suit is polished fine,
God sees through all the glamour,
As deeds are your battle line.

Your soul's what goes to heaven,
You are what gets you there,
Now dress your life accordingly,
God doesn't care what you wear.

HOW GOD CARES FOR US

By Eugene Pacetti

'Tis fall the air is crisp,
The leaves are colored bright,
The artist's hand is God,
How they glimmer in the light.

Soon the leaves will fall,
Bare arms reach toward the sky,
As if to say we thank you God,
Now they appear to die.

A blanket of snow will cover the land,
And the earth entombed will lay.
To await God's shining sun,
And the land will rise this day.

As Christ was dead,
And entombed in a hole,
Truly God's son arose,
To cleanse our sinful soul.

The sun will come to warm the earth,
Life will rise through out the land,
Flowers and trees, they all will bloom,
By the gardener we know, God's hand.

When all the fruit is harvested,
The cold will be our test,
When the cycle is complete,
The earth will lie and rest.

God cares for us as He does the earth,
He lets us grow to our own will,
What type of harvest will you reap?
Lost crop, or with God your heart to fill.

IT'S THE DAWNING OF A BRAND NEW DAY

By Eugene Pacetti

In the small town of Chapel Hill, a group of wonderful, God loving people were starting a new church. My wife, God love her, is a member of this group. They desire to reach out into the community and bring people to Christ. I wrote this poem for my wife and the new church, which is growing by leaps and bounds. God is working here.

It's the dawning of a brand new day,
A miracle is being spun,
And God is spinning it his own way,
All that join will now be one.

God will lead this chosen flock,
And on their knees they will fall to pray.
Listen to the ticking clock,
It's the dawning of a brand new day.

Lift up your head and sing his praises,
Then listen to what God has to say.
With all His love our hopes he raises,
It's the dawning of a brand new day.

We will spread his word through out the town,
God's word we'll let the people weigh,
Then listen to the beautiful sound.
It's the dawning of a brand new day.

All who come will feel God's love,
The Bible guides us, open will lay.
His flock receives a pure white dove.
It's the dawning of a brand new day.

Tell the world, God gave His son,
He died to wash our sins away,
Christ unites us now as one.
It's the dawning of a brand new day.

As you go out and spread God's love,
Tell all that Jesus is the way,
To heaven and the Lord above.
It's the dawning of a brand new day.

THE HOPEFUL CHRISTMAS

By Eugene Pacetti

Christmas is all around us,
The season of good cheer.
The time when children never fuss,
'Cause Santa Claus is near.

On everyone's lips a happy greeting,
As no one notices color or race.
Joy in the air upon their meeting,
And on all a cheerful face.

If goodwill this year could forever last,
There'd be no anger, war or strife.
There'd be a peaceful future, a forgotten past,
Except for the day when Christ was life.

May the New Year bring peace upon this earth.
And let men be blessed with joy and cheer.
Let there be love, goodwill and mirth.
Throughout mankind, both far and near.

This Christmas wish I extend to you,
May peace prevail, may days be blessed,
May happiness reign and brotherhood too.
Merry Christmas to all, the season's best.

Section Four:

Along The Way

The following collection of poems, stories and tidbits we've seen from various sources but have unknown authors to us. We've placed them in this special section, titled "Along the Way," because somewhere along the way they have impacted our lives in a special way and we hope they do the same for you.

IF I COULD

I've seen this poem in several places, and it truly deserves to be shared. I called it "IF I COULD"

If I could catch a rainbow,
I would do it just for you,
And share with you it's beauty,
On days you're feeling blue.
If I could build a mountain,
You could call your very own,
A place to find serenity,
A place to be alone.
If I could take your troubles,
I'd toss them in the sea,
But all these things I'm finding,
Are impossible for me.
I can not build a mountain,
Or catch a rainbow fair,
But let me be what I know best,
A friend that's always there

THE REDNECK LOVE POEM

As Valentine's Day approached, I saw this poem on the Internet. Notice the spelling and the pronunciation through out the poem. It just tickled my ribs and I hope you have fun reading it.

Collards are green
My dog's name is blue,
And I'm so lucky,
To have a sweet thang like you.

Yore hair is like cornsilk,
A flappin in the breeze.
Softer than Blue's,
With out all them fleas.

You move like the bass,
That excite me in May.
You ain't got no scales,
But, I luv you anyway.

Yo're as satisy'n as okry,
Jist a-fry'n in the pan.
Yo're as fragrant as "snuff",
Right out of the can.

You have some'a yore teeth,
For which I am proud.
I hold my head high,
When we'uns in a crowd.

On special occasions,
When you shave under yore arms,
Well, I'm in hawg heaven,
And awed by yore charms.

Still them fellers at work,
They all want to know,
What I did to deserve,
Such a purdy young doe.
Like a good roll of duck tape,
Yo're there for yore man,
To patch up life's troubles,
And fix what you can.

Yo're as cute as a June bug,
A-buzzin' overhead.
You ain't mean like those far (fire) ants,
I found in my bed.

Cut from the best cloth,
Like a plaid flannel shirt,
You spark up my life,
More than a fresh load of dirt.

When you hold me real tight,
Like a padded gun rack.
My life is complete.
Ain't nottin I lack.

Yore complexion, it's perfection,
Like the best vinyl sidin',
Despite all the years,
Yore age, it keeps hidin'.

Me "n" you's like a moon pie,
With a RC cold drank.
We go together, like a skunk goes with stank.

Some men, they buy chocolates,
For Valentine's Day.
They git it at Walmart,
It's romantic that way.

Some men git roses,
On that special day.
From the cooler at Krogers,
That's impressive I say.
Some men buy fine diamonds,
From a flea market booth.
"Diamonds are forever,"
They explain, suave and couth.

But for this man, honey,
These won't do,
Cause yo're too special,
You sweet thang, you.

I got you a gift,
Without taste nor odor,
More useful than diamonds,
IT'S A NEW TROLLIN MOTOR.

'TWAS THE NIGHT BEFORE EXAMS

This poem was found tacked on a college bulletin board the day before finals.

"Twas the night before finals
And all through the college
The students were praying
For last minute knowledge

Most were quite sleepy,
But none touched their beds,
While visions of essays,
Danced in their heads.

Out in the taverns,
A few were still drinking,
And hoping that liquor
Would loosen up their thinking.

In my own apartment,
I had been pacing,
And dreading exams,
I soon would be facing.

My roommate was speechless,
His nose in his books,
And my comments to him
Drew unfriendly looks.

I drained all the coffee,
And brewed a new pot,
No longer caring
My nerves were all shot.

I stared at my notes,
But my thoughts were muddy,
My eyes went ablur,
I just couldn't study

"Some pizza might help,"
I said with a shiver,
But each place I called
Refused to deliver.

I'd nearly concluded,
That life was too cruel,
With futures depending
On grades had in school.

When all of a sudden,
Our door opened wide,
And Patron Saint Put it Off
Ambled inside.

Her spirit was careless,
Her manner was mellow,
Her voice was smooth,
As she started to bellow.

"What kind of student
Would make such a fuss,
To toss back at teachers
What they tossed at us?"

"On cliff notes! On crib notes!
On tests and exams,
On wingit and slingit,
And study and crams.

Her message delivered,
She vanished from sight,
But we heard her laughing
Outside in the night.

"Your teachers have pegged you,
So just do your best.
Happy finals to all,
And to all a good test.

SPECIAL POEM FOR SENIORS

I came across this poem on the internet and quickly thought, "This is me." I wonder how many other senior citizens take a lot of pills. Is this you?

A row of bottles on my shelf,
Caused me to analyze myself.

One yellow pill I have to pop,
Goes to my heart so it won't stop.

A little white one that I take,
Goes to my hands so they won't shake.

The blue ones that I use a lot,
Tell me I'm happy when I'm not.

The purple pill goes to my brain,
And tells me that I have no pain.

The capsules tell me not to wheeze,
Or cough or choke or even sneeze.

The red ones, smallest of them all,
Go to my blood so I won't fall.

The orange ones, very big and bright,
Prevent my leg cramps in the night.

Such an array of brilliant pills,
Helping to cure all kinds of ills.

But what I'd really like to know…
Is what tells each one where to go!

I HAVE A FRIEND

This poem was handed to me and I was asked to read it to a group. I don't know who wrote it, but I'd like to share it with you. It has a great meaning.

Around the corner I have a friend.
In this great city that has no end.

Yet the days go by and weeks rush on,
And before I know it, a year has gone.

And I never see my old friend's face,
For life is a swift and terrible race.

He knows I like him just as well,
As in the days when I rang his bell.

And he rang mine, but we were younger then,
And now we are busy, tired men.

Tired of playing a foolish game,
Tired of trying to make a name.

"Tomorrow," I say! I will call on Jim,
Just to show that I'm thinking of him.

But tomorrow comes and tomorrow goes,
And the distance between us grows and grows.

Around the corner, yet miles away,
"Here's a telegram sir," "Jim died today."

And that's what we get and deserve in the end,
Around the corner, a vanished friend.

Remember to always say what you mean. If you care about someone, tell them. Don't be afraid to express yourself. Reach out and tell someone what they mean to you. Because when you decide that it's the right time it might be too late. Seize the day. Never have regrets. And most importantly, stay close to your friends and family, for they have helped make you the person that you are today.

A CHILDS DREAM

I found this poem posted in a men's basketball locker room. The emphasis was that young children watch athletes and hold them up as heroes, hoping that someday they can be like them. Maybe all athletes, especially college and professional, should receive a copy of this poem. This could be anyone a child looks up to. Could this someone be you?

There's a child's eyes upon you,
And they're watching night and day.
There are little ears that quickly
Take in every word you say.

There are little hands all eager
To do anything you do.
And a little child who's dreaming,
Of the day they'll be like you.

You're the little child's idol,
You're the wisest of the wise.
In this little mind about you,
No suspicions do arise.

This child believes in you devoutly,
Holds that all you say and do.
They will say and do it your way,
When they're grown up like you.

There's a wide eyed little child,
Who believes you're always right.
And their eyes are always open,
And they watch both day and night.

You are setting an example,
Everyday in all you do.
For the little child who's waiting,
To grow up to be like you.

WHEN I WHINE

Do you complain about things in your life? Do you wish you had more? Do you envy others for what they have? You may be blessed and not even know it. Check this poem out that came across the internet with a note to pass it on to remind us how blessed we are.

Today, upon a bus,
I saw a girl with golden hair,
I looked at her and sighed
and wished I was as fair.

When suddenly she rose to leave,
I saw her hobble down the aisle.
She had one leg and used a crutch,
But as she passed, she passed a smile.

Oh, God, forgive me when I whine
I have two legs, the world is mine

I stopped to buy some candy,
The lad who sold it had such charm,
I talked with him a while, he seemed so very glad,
If I were late it'd do no harm.

And as I left, he said to me,
"Thank you, you've been so kind.
It's nice to talk with folks like you.
You see," he said, "I'm blind.

Oh, God, forgive me when I whine,
I have two eyes, the world is mine.

Later while walking down the street,
I saw a child with eyes of blue,
He stood and watched the others play,
He did not know what to do.

I stopped a moment and then turned I said,
"Why don't you join the others, dear?"
He looked ahead without a word,
And then I knew, he couldn't hear.

Oh, God, forgive me when I whine,
I have two ears, the world is mine.

With feet to take me where I'd go,
With eyes to see the sunset's glow,
With ears to hear what I would know.

Oh, God, forgive me when I whine.
I've been blessed indeed, the world is mine.

If this poem makes you feel like I felt, read it to all your friends. After all, it's a simple reminder. We have ever so much to be thankful for.

Sorrow looks back
Worry looks around
Faith looks up.

GREAT TRUTHS IN OUR LIVES

Ten Great Truths That Little Children Have Learned
1. No matter how hard you try, you can't baptize cats.
2. When your mom is mad at your dad, don't let her brush your hair.
3. Never ask your 3-year old brother to hold a tomato.
4. You can't trust dogs to watch your food.
5. If your sister hits you, don't hit her back. They always catch the second person.
6. Don't sneeze when someone is cutting your hair.
7. Never hold a Dust-Buster and a cat at the same time.
8. You can't hide a piece of broccoli in a glass of milk.
9. Don't wear polka-dot underwear under white shorts.
10. The best place to be when you're sad is grandpa's lap.

Great Truths That Adults Have Learned

Raising teenagers is like nailing jelly to a tree. Wrinkles don't hurt. Families are like fudge… mostly sweet with a few nuts. Today's mighty oak is just yesterday's nut that held its ground. Laughing is good exercise. It's like jogging on the inside. Middle age is when you choose your cereal for the fiber, not the toy.

Great Truths About Growing Old

Growing old is mandatory; growing up is optional. Forget the health food. I need all the preservatives I can get. When you fall down, you wonder what else you can do while you're down there. You're getting old when you get the same sensation from a rocking chair that you once got from a roller coaster. It's frustrating when you know all the answers but nobody bothers to ask you the questions. Time may be a great healer, but it's a lousy beautician. Wisdom comes with age, but sometimes age comes alone.

The Four Stages Of Life
You believe in Santa Claus
You don't believe in Santa Claus

You are Santa Claus.
You look like Santa Claus.

What Is Success?
At age 4 success is…..not piddling in your pants.
At age 12 success is…..having friends
At age 17 success is…..having a drivers license
At age 35 success is…..having money
At age 50 success is…..having money
At age 70 success is…..having friends
At age 75 success is…..having friends
At age 80 success is…..not piddling in your pants.

ALWAYS REMEMBER TO FORGET THE TROUBLES THAT PASS YOUR WAY; BUT NEVER FORGET THE BLESSINGS THAT COME EACH DAY.

HAVE YOU EVER WONDERED WHAT COLOR TO PAINT?

What would look good in the kitchen or what color should we paint our bedroom? Should we brighten up the bathroom or let's paint the den. Here are some tips on what color does for you and how it makes you feel.

RED..........Encourages energy and determination and INVIGORATES its environment. Red is associated with good health.

ORANGE.....Stimulates the appetite and conversation. Orange is associated with happiness, courage and success.

PINK..........A tranquilizing color that zaps energy. It soothes and nurtures, while suppressing anger, antagonism and anxiety.

YELLOW.....Suggest cheer and increases energy. It cultivates enthusiasm, playfulness, creativity and optimism.

BRIGHT YELLOW.....Reflects a lot of light, causing excessive eye stimulation.

WHITE.....Surfaces reflect 80% of light.

BLACK.....Surfaces reflect only 5% of light.

BLUE.......An appetite suppressant. Weight loss programs suggest putting food on blue plates. Blue doesn't exist in any significant quantity as a natural color, so it triggers no automatic appetite response.

GREEN.....Provides balance and refreshes. Because it is the color of spring, it is associated with growth and plenitude.

HOW A MAN THINKS

Ever wonder what goes through a man's mind when he thinks he's so macho. Here are a few items on the thinking of a man.

How many men does it take to open a can of beer?
NONE. It should be open when she brings it to you.

Why is a Laundromat a really bad place to pick up a woman?
Because a woman who can't even afford a washing machine will probably never be able to support you.

Why do women have smaller feet than men?
It's one of those "evolutionary things" that allows them to stand closer to the kitchen sink.

How do you know when a woman is about to say something smart?
When she starts a sentence with "A man once told me…"

How do you fix a woman's watch?
You don't. There's a clock on the oven.

If your dog is barking at the back door and your wife is yelling at the front door, who do you let in first?
The dog of course. He'll shut up once you let him in

What's worse than a male chauvinist pig?
A woman who won't do as she's told.

I married a Miss Right.
I just didn't know her first name was always.

Scientists have discovered a food that diminishes a woman's sex drive by 90%.
It's called a wedding cake.

Women will never be equal to men until they can walk down the street with a bald head and a beer gut and still think they are sexy.

In the beginning God made the earth and took a little rest.
Then God created man and took a little rest.
Then God created woman.
Then God, man nor woman never rested any more.

MID – LIFE

There's been a few shows on TV lately that went on and on about how mid-life is a great time for women. Whether your pushing 40, 50, 60 (or maybe even just pushing your luck) here are some thoughts you probably can relate to.

Mid-life is when the growth of hair on our legs slows down. This gives us plenty of time to care for you newly acquired mustache.

In mid- life women no longer have upper arms, we have wing spans. We are no longer women in sleeveless shirt; we are flying squirrels in drag.

Mid-life is when you can stand naked in front of a mirror and you can see your rear without turning around.

Mid-life is when you go for a mammogram and you realize that this is the only time someone will ask you to appear topless.

Mid-life is when you want to grab every firm young lovely in a tube top and scream, "Listen honey, even the Roman empire fell and those will too.

Mid-life brings wisdom to know that life throws us curves and we're sitting on our biggest ones.

Mid-life is when you look at your- know-it-all teenager and think, "For this I have stretch marks?"

In mid-life your memory starts to go. In fact the only thing we can retain is water.

Mid-life means that your Body By Jake now includes Legs by Rand McNally –more red and blue lines than an accurately scaled map of Wisconsin.

Mid-life means that you become more reflective…You start pondering the "big" questions. What is life? Why am I here? How much Healthy choice ice cream can I eat before it's no longer a healthy choice?

But mid-life also brings with it an appreciation for what is important. We realize that breast sag, hips expand and chin double, but our loved ones make the journey worthwhile. Would any of you trade the knowledge that you have now, for the body you had way back when? Maybe our bodies simply have to expand to hold all the wisdom and love we've acquired. That's my philosophy and I'm sticking to it.

REASONS WHY IT'S GREAT TO BE A GUY

Phone conversations are over in 30 seconds flat.

A five-day vacation requires only one suitcase.

You can open all your own jars

Dry cleaners and hair cutters don't rob you blind.

You can go to the bathroom without a support group.

You can leave the motel bed unmade.

You get extra credit for the slightest act of thoughtfulness.

Wedding plans take care of themselves.

If someone forgets to invite you to something, he or she can still be your friend.

Your underwear is $10 for a three pack.

If you are 34 and single, nobody notices.

Everything on your face stays its original color.

You can quietly enjoy a car ride from the passenger's seat.

Three pairs of shoes are more than enough.

Car mechanics tell you the truth.

You can quietly watch a game with your buddies for hours without ever thinking: "He must be mad at me."

Gray hair and wrinkles only add character.

Wedding dress-$2,000, Tuxedo rental – 75 bucks.

You can drop by to see a friend without bringing a little gift.

You are not expected to know the names of more than 5 colors.

You know which way to turn a nut on a bolt.

You almost never have strap problems in public.

Wrinkles are non-existent in your clothes.

The same hairstyle lasts for years, maybe decades

You don't have to shave below your neck.

One wallet and one pair of shoes, one color, all seasons.

CRACKED POT

This came across my desk via the internet. I don't know who wrote it but it has a good message that should be shared.

An elderly Chinese woman had two large pots, each hung on the ends of a pole, which she carried across her neck

One of the pots had a crack in it while the other pot was perfect and always delivered a full portion of water, at the end of the long walk from the stream to the house, the cracked pot arrived only half full. For a full two years this went on daily, with the woman bringing home only one and a half pots of water. Of course the perfect pot proud of its accomplishments. But the poor cracked pot was ashamed of its own imperfection, and miserable that it could only do half of what it had been made to do.

After two years of what it perceived to be bitter failure, it spoke to the woman one day by the stream. "I am ashamed of myself, because this crack in my side causes water to leak out all the way back to your house.

The old woman smiled, "Did you notice that there are flowers on your side of the path, but not on the other side?" "That's because I have always known about your flaw, so I planted flower seeds on your side of the path, and every day while we walk back, you watered them. For two years I have been able to pick these beautiful flowers to decorate the table. Without you being just the way you are, there would not be this beauty to grace the house."

Each of us has our own unique flaw. But it's the cracks and flaws we each have that make our lives together so very interesting and rewarding. You've just got to take each person for what they are and look for the good in them.

SO....to all my "crackpot" friends, have a great day and remember to smell the flowers on your side of the path!!!

REMEMBER THE GOOD OLD DAYS

Being a kid in the early 50's this appealed to me, so I thought I'd pass it on to you.

Were you a kid in the mid-60's or earlier? Everybody makes fun of our childhood! Comedians make jokes. Grand kids snicker. People in their 20's shudder and say "EeeeeW!" But was our childhood really all that bad? Read and judge for yourself:

In 1953 the US population was less than 150 million…Yet you knew more people then, and knew them better…And that was good.

The average annual salary was under $3,000….yet our parents could put some of it away for a rainy day and still live a decent life (sure they didn't have to pay for satellite TV, VCR's, DVD's, cell phones, boom boxes, yadda yadda)…And that was good.

A loaf of bread cost about 15 cents…But it was safe for a five-year-old to skate to the store and buy one…And that was good. Prime-Time meant I Love Lucy, Ozzie and Harriet, Gunsmoke and Lassie…So nobody ever heard of ratings or filters…And that was good.

We didn't have air-conditioning…So the windows stayed up and half a dozen mothers ran outside when you fell off your bike because they heard it…And that was good.Your teacher was Miss Matthews or Mrs. Logan or Mr. Adkins…But not Ms Becky or Mr. Dan …And that was good.

The only hazardous material you knew about…Was a patch of grass burrs around the light pole at the corner…And that was good. You loved to climb into a fresh bed…Because sheets were dried on the clothesline…And that was good.

People generally lived in the same hometown with their relatives… So "child care" meant grandparents or aunts and uncles…And that was good. Parents were respected and their rules were law…Children did not talk back…And that was good.

TV was in black and white …But all outdoors was in God's glorious color…And that was certainly good. Your dad knew how to adjust everybody's carburetor...And the dad next door knew how to adjust all the TV knobs...And that was very good.

Your grandma grew snap beans in the back yard...And chickens behind the garage...And that was definitely good. And just when you were about to do something really bad...Chances were you'd run into your dad's high school coach...Or the nosy old lady from up the street... Or little sister's piano teacher...Or somebody from church...ALL of whom knew your parents phone number...And your first name...And even that was good.

Can you remember Nancy Drew, The Hardy Boys, Laurel and Hardy, Abbott and Costello, Sky King, Little Lulu comics, Brenda Starr, Howdy Doody and the Peanut Gallery, The Lone Ranger, The Shadow Knows, Nellie Belle, Roy and Dale, Trigger and Buttermilk, as well as the sound of a "reel" mower on Saturday morning, and summers filled with bike rides, playing in cowboy land, playing hide and seek and kick-the-can and Simon says, baseball games, amateur shows at the local theater before the Saturday matinee, bowling and visits to the pool...And eating kool-aid powder with sugar, and wax lips and bubble gum cigars.

Didn't that feel good, just to go back and say, YEAH, I remember that! AND WAS IT REALLY THAT LONG AGO!!!

I RESIGN

Across the waves of the Internet came this funny little story. I'm sure we all have felt this way at one time or another.

I am hereby officially tendering my resignation as an adult. I have decided I would like to accept the responsibilities of an 8-year old.

I want to go to McDonald's and think it's a four star restaurant.

I want to sail sticks across a fresh mud puddle and make a sidewalk with rocks,

I want to think M&Ms are better than money because you can eat them.

I want to lie under a big oak tree and run a lemonade stand with my friends on a hot summer's day.

I want to return to a time when life was simple. When all you knew were colors, multiplication tables, and nursery rhymes, but that didn't bother you, because you didn't know what you didn't know and you didn't care. All you knew was to be happy because you were blissfully unaware of all the things that should make you worried or upset.

I want to think the world is fair.

That everyone is honest and good.

I want to believe that anything is possible.

I want to be oblivious to the complexities of life and be excited by the little things again.

I want to live simple again.

I don't want my day to consist of computer crashes, mountains of paperwork, depressing news, how to survive more days in the month than there is money in the bank, doctor bills, gossip, illness, and loss of loved ones.

I want to believe in the power of smiles, hugs, a kind word, truth, justice, peace, dreams, the imagination, mankind, and making angels in the snow.

So…here's my checkbook and my car keys, my credit card bills and my 401K statements. I am officially resigning from adulthood.

And if you want to discuss this further, you'll have to catch me first, cause….."TAG! YOU'RE IT."

LIFE LESSONS

Here are five really short stories. Each has an important lesson to make you think about the way we treat people. What would you have done if you were in their place?

THE CLEANING LADY

During my second month of college, our professor gave us a pop quiz. I was a conscientious student and had breezed through the questions until I read the last one:

"What is the first name of the woman who cleans the school?"

Surely this was some kind of joke. I had seen the cleaning woman several times. She was tall, dark-haired and in her 50's, but how would I know her name? I handed in my paper, leaving the last question blank. Just before class ended, one student asked if the last question would count toward our quiz grade.

"Absolutely," said the professor. "In your careers, you will meet many people. All are significant. They deserve your attention and care, even if all you do is smile and say "hello."

I've never forgotten that lesson. I also learned her name was Dorothy.

PICKUP IN THE RAIN

One night, at 11:30p.m., an older African American woman was standing on the side of an Alabama highway trying to endure a lashing rainstorm. Her car had broken down and she desperately needed a ride. Soaking wet, she decided to flag down the next car. A young white man stopped to help her, generally unheard of in those conflict-filled 1960s. The man took her to safety, helped her get assistance and put her into a taxicab.

She seemed to be in a big hurry, but wrote down his address and thanked him. Seven day went by and a knock came on the man's door. To his surprise, a giant console color TV was delivered to his home. A special note was attached. It read:

Thank you so much for assisting me on the highway
the other night. The rain drenched not only my clothes,

but also my spirits. Then you came along. Because of you, I was able to make it to my dying husband's bedside just before he passed away...God bless you for helping me and unselfishly serving others.

Sincerely,
Mrs. Nat King Cole

ALWAYS REMEMBER THOSE WHO SERVE

In the days when an ice cream sundae cost much less, a 10-year –old boy entered a hotel coffee shop and sat at a table. A waitress put a glass of water in front of him.

"How much is an ice cream sundae?" he asked.

"Fifty cents," replied the waitress. The little boy pulled his hand out of his pocket and studied the coins in it.

"Well, how much is a plain dish of ice cream?" he inquired. By now more people were waiting for a table and the waitress was growing impatient.

"Thirty-five cents," she brusquely replied. The little boy again counted his coins.

"I'll have the plain ice cream," he said. The waitress brought the ice cream, put the bill on the table and walked away. The boy finished his ice cream, paid the cashier and left. When the waitress came back, she began to cry as she wiped down the table. There, placed neatly beside the empty dish, were two nickels and five pennies.

You see he couldn't have the sundae, because he had to have enough to leave her a tip.

THE OBSTACLE IN OUR PATH

In ancient times a King had a boulder placed on a roadway. Then he hid himself and watched to see if anyone would remove the huge rock. Some of the King's wealthiest merchants and courtiers came by and simply walked around it. Many loudly blamed the King for not keeping the roads clear, but none did anything about getting the stone out of the way.

Then a peasant came along carrying a load of vegetables. Upon approaching the boulder, the peasant laid down his burden and tried to move the stone to the side of the road. After much pushing and straining, he finally succeeded. After the peasant picked up his load of vegetables, he noticed a purse lying in the road where the boulder had been. The purse contained many gold coins and a note from the King indicating that the gold was for the person who removed the boulder from the roadway. The peasant learned what many of us never understand!

Every obstacle presents an opportunity to improve our condition.

Giving When It Counts

Many years ago, when I worked as a volunteer at a hospital, I got to know a little girl named Liz who was suffering from a rare and serious disease. Her only chance of recovery appeared to be a blood transfusion from her 5-year old brother, who had miraculously survived the same disease and had developed the antibodies needed to combat the illness. The doctor explained the situation to her little brother, and asked the little boy if he would be willing to give his blood to his sister.

I saw him hesitate for only a moment before taking a deep breath and saying, "Yes I'll do it if it will save her." As the transfusion progressed, he lay in bed next to his sister and smiled, as we all did, seeing the color returning to her cheek. Then his face grew pale and his smile faded.

He looked up at the doctor and asked with a trembling voice, "Will I start to die right away?"

Being young, the little boy had misunderstood the doctor, he thought he was going to have to give his sister all of his blood in order to save her.

Will these stories change the way you treat people?

THE BEGINNING...

As you read, does this sound familiar? Where do you fit in? I was there from start to finish. A lady gave me this to read in church. Everyone enjoyed it, so I thought I'd share it with you.

In the beginning God populated the earth with broccoli and cauliflower and spinach, green and yellow and red vegetables of all kinds, so man and woman would live long and healthy lives. Then using God's great gifts, Satan created Ben and Jerry's and Krispy Crème...

And Satan said, "You want chocolate with that?" And Man said "yea." And woman said, "And another one with sprinkles." And they gained 10 pounds.

And God created the healthful yogurt that woman might keep the figure that man found so fair. And Satan brought forth white flour from the wheat, and sugar from the cane, and combined them. Woman went from size two to size 16.

So God said, "Try my fresh green salad." And Satan presented Thousand-Island Dressing and Garlic toast on the side. And man and woman unfastened their belts following the repast.

God then said. "I have sent you heart healthy vegetables and olive oil in which to cook them." And Satan brought forth deep fried fish and chicken- fried steak so big it needed its own platter. And man gained more weight and his cholesterol went through the roof.

God then brought running shoes so that his children might loose those extra pounds. And Satan gave cable TV with a remote control so man would not have to toil changing the channels. And man and woman laughed and cried before the flickering light and gained pounds.

Then God brought forth the potato, naturally low in fat and brimming with nutrition. And Satan peeled off the healthful skin and sliced the starchy center into chips and deep-fried them. And Man gained pounds.

God then gave lean beef so man might consume fewer calories and still satisfy his appetite. And Satan created McDonald's and it's 99-cent double cheeseburger. Then he said, "You want fries with that?" And man replied, "Yea! And super size 'em." And Satan said, "It is good." And man went into cardiac arrest.

God sighed and created quadruple bypass surgery. And Satan created HMOs.

Look in the mirror. Isn't it time to get Satan out of our lives???

RELIGIOUS FUED

This will tickle your funny bone. I don't know who wrote it, as it came to me via email.

There was a feud between the pastor and the choir director of a small Southern Baptist Church. It seems the first hint of trouble came when the Pastor preached on "DEDICATING YOURSELF TO SERVICE." The choir director chose to sing, "I SHALL NOT BE MOVED."

Trying to believe it was a coincidence, the Pastor put the incident behind him. The next Sunday he preached on, "GIVING." The choir squirmed as the director led them in the hymn: "JESUS PAID IT ALL."

By this time the Pastor was losing his temper. Sunday morning attendance swelled as the tension between the two built. A large crowd showed up the next Sunday to hear his sermon on, "THE SIN OF GOSSIPING." Would you believe the choir director selected: "I LOVE TO TELL THE STORY." There was no turning back.

The following Sunday the Pastor told the congregation that unless something changed he was considering resignation. The entire church gasped when the choir director led them in, "WHY NOT TONIGHT." Truthfully, no one was surprised when the Pastor resigned a week later explaining that Jesus had led him there and Jesus was leading him away. The choir director could not resist, the choir sang: "WHAT A FRIEND WE HAVE IN JESUS."

A CHILD'S RESPONSE

Here's how a few children responded to the meaning of some Bible stories........

STORY OF ELIJAH

The Sunday school teacher was carefully explaining the story of Elijah the Prophet and the false prophets of Baal. She explained how Elijah built the alter, put wood upon it, cut a steer in pieces, and laid it upon the altar. And then, Elijah commanded the people of God to fill four barrels of water and pour it over the altar. He had them do this four times." Now," said the teacher, "can anyone in the class tell me why the Lord would have Elijah pour water over the steer on the altar?" A little girl in the back of the room started waving her hand, "I know, I know," she said, "to make the gravy!"

LOT'S WIFE

The Sunday school teacher was describing how Lot's wife looked back and turned into a pillar of salt, when little Johnny interrupted, "My mummy looked back once, while she was DRIVING," he announced triumphantly, "and she turned into a telephone pole!"

DID NOAH FISH?

A Sunday school teacher asked, "Johnny, do you think Noah did a lot of fishing when he was on the Ark?" "No," replied Johnny. "How could he, with just two worms."

HIGHER POWER

A Sunday school teacher said to her children, "We have been learning how powerful kings and queens were in Bible times. But, there is a higher power. Can anybody tell me what it is?" One child blurted out, "Aces!"

THE LORD IS MY SHEPARD

A Sunday school teacher decided to have her young class memorize one of the most quoted passages in the Bible; Psalm 23. She gave the youngsters a month to learn the verse. Little Bobby was excited about the task. But, he just couldn't remember the Psalm. After much practice, he could barely get past the first line. On the day that the kids were scheduled to recite Psalm 23 in front of the congregation, Bobby was so nervous. When it was his turn, he stepped up to the microphone and said proudly, "The Lord is my shepherd and that's all I need to know."

GOD HAS A POSITIVE ANSWER

God's answer to what you say.
You say: "It's impossible"
God says: All things are possible.
(Luke 18:27)

You say: "I'm too tired"
God says: I will give you rest
(Matthew 11:28-30)

You say: "Nobody really loves me.
God says: I love you.
(John 3:16 & John 3:34)

You say: "I can't go on"
God says: My grace is sufficient
(II Corinthians 12:9 & Psalm 91:15)

You say: "I can't figure things out"
God says: I will direct your steps
(Proverbs 3:5-6)

You say: "I can't do it"
God says: You can do all things
(Philippians 4:13)

You say: "I'm not able"
God says: I am able
(II Corinthians 9:8)

You say: "It's not worth it"
God says: It will be worth it
(Roman 8:28)

You say: "I can't forgive myself"
God says: I forgive you
(I John 1:9 & Romans 8:1)

You say: I can't manage"
God says: I will supply all your needs
(Philippians 4:19)

You say: "I'm afraid"
God says: I have not given you a spirit of fear
(II Timothy 1:7)

You say: "I'm always worried and frustrated"
God says: Cast all your cares on ME
(I Peter 5:7)

You say: "I'm not smart enough"
God says: I give you wisdom
(I Corinthians 1:30)

You say: "I feel all alone"
God says: I will never leave you
(Hebrews 13:5)

A FEW THOUGHTS FOR TODAY
Forget injuries
Never forget kindness
A day hemmed in prayer seldom unravels
As long as there are tests
There will always be prayer in school
Prayer should be our first resource
Not our last resort

MY OATH TO YOU
When you are sad.......................I will dry your tears
When you are scared...................I will comfort your fears
When you are worried.................I will give you hope

When you are confused.................I will help you cope
And when you are lost..................And can't see the light
I shall be your beacon..................Shining ever so bright
This is my oath...........................I pledge till the end.
Why you may ask?.....................Because you're my friends
Signed: GOD

MARY HAD A LITTLE LAMB
Author Unknown

Every one has heard the poem of Mary Had A Little Lamb. Here are two versions that came across my desk and I'd like to share them with you.

Mary had a little lamb,
His fleece was white as snow.
And everywhere that Mary went,
The lamb was sure to go.
He followed her to school each day,
It was OK by the rule.
It made the children laugh and play,
To have the lamb at school.

VERSION II
Then the rules all changed one day,
Illegal it became;
To bring the lamb of God to school,
Or even speak His name.
Every day got worse and worse;
And days turned into years.
Instead of hearing children laugh,
We heard the shots and tears.
What must we do to stop the crime,
That's in our schools today?
Let's let the lamb come back to school,
And teach our kids to pray.

THE LEGEND OF THE SAND DOLLAR

There are several versions of this poem, often found on postcards, greeting cards, plaques and gift store items. None listed an author. This version was sited as being in the Seattle Post Intelligencer, April 6, 1966.

There's a pretty little legend,
That I would like to tell,
Of the birth and death of Jesus,
Found in this lowly little shell.

If you examine closely,
You'll see that you find here,
Four nail holes and a fifth one,
Made by a Roman's spear.

On one side the Easter lily,
Its center is the star,
That appeared unto the shepherds,
And led them from a far.

The Christmas poinsettia,
Etched on the other side,
Reminds us of His birthday,
Our happy Christmastide.

Now break the center open,
And here you will release,
The five white doves awaiting,
To spread good will and peace.

This simple little symbol,
Christ left for you and me,
To help us spread His Gospel,
Through all eternity.

MERRY CHRISTMAS FROM HEAVEN

It was late December when my wife's sister died and the Christmas season now seemed to have little meaning. The joy was taken out of joyful and for us it was not the season to be merry. Polly had left us, her smiling face and silly giggle would be no more. How could we cope during this special time of year? Then I came upon this poem. It made Christmas more meaningful as we celebrated the birth of Jesus. We'd like to share this with you.

I still hear the sounds,
I still see the lights,
I still feel your love,
On cold wintry nights.

I still share your hopes
And all of your cares.
I'll even remind you
To please say your prayers

I just want to tell you,
You still make me proud
To stand head and shoulders
Above all the crowd.

Keep trying each moment,
To stay in his grace.
I came here before you,
To help set your place.

You don't have to be
Perfect all the time.
He forgives you the slip,
If you continue the climb.

To my family and friends,
Please be thankful today,
I'm still close beside you,
In a new special way.

I love you all dearly,
Now don't shed a tear,
Cause I'm spending my Christmas
With Jesus this year.